Transformational Leadership in Special Education

Leading the IEP Team

Kirby Lentz

ROWMAN & LITTLEFIELD EDUCATION

A division of
ROWMAN & LITTLEFIELD PUBLISHERS, INC.
Lanham • New York • Toronto • Plymouth, UK

Published by Rowman & Littlefield Education
A division of Rowman & Littlefield Publishers, Inc.
A wholly owned subsidiary of The Rowman & Littlefield Publishing Group, Inc.
4501 Forbes Boulevard, Suite 200, Lanham, Maryland 20706
www.rowman.com

10 Thornbury Road, Plymouth PL6 7PP, United Kingdom

British Library Cataloguing in Publication Information Available

Library of Congress Cataloging-in-Publication Data

Lentz, Kirby.
  Transformational leadership in special education : leading the IEP team / Kirby Lentz.
    p. cm.
  Summary: "Using the principles of transformational leadership, IEP teams become
effective tools to ensure student success and achievements. There is a difference of
teams that are simply chaired and those that are lead. Teams with transformational
leaders promote the best efforts of all participants including parents and students to
effectively deliver special education services that meet real student outcomes. Using
a step-by-step approach to developing the IEP, improving team function and producing
Great IEPs, schools and districts can demonstrate special education effectiveness
through success and achievement of students"— Provided by publisher.
  ISBN 978-1-61048-512-8 (hardback) — ISBN 978-1-61048-513-5 (paper) —
ISBN 978-1-61048-514-2 (ebook)
  1. Children with disabilities—Education--United States. 2. Individualized education
programs—United States—Management. 3. Educational leadership. I. Title.
  LC4031.L44 2012
  371.90973—dc23

                                                                        2012006746

∞™ The paper used in this publication meets the minimum requirements of American
National Standard for Information Sciences—Permanence of Paper for Printed Library
Materials, ANSI/NISO Z39.48-1992.

Printed in the United States of America

In deepest gratitude to and inspiration from my wife, BJ

In honor of

My mother, Marjorie K. Lentz

My children, Ryan, Katrina, Griffin, and their families

In memory of

My father, Dr. Robert T. Lentz (1910–1998)

My mother-in law, Helen L. Wall (1911–2011)

Contents

List of Figures

Preface

This writing is an effort to help special education administrators, school psychologists, and others who chair and lead the crucial special education IEP team meetings to know how to do just that. For over thirty-five years it has always been assumed that school officials know how to lead the IEP team and to chair this team meeting, yet there are no known classes or written guides that help school professionals to lead, not just conduct, the IEP team meeting in a purposeful and meaningful way.

The author did not know how to lead or chair the IEP team meeting either and thought, at the beginning of forty years in education, that anyone could introduce a meeting and it would somehow run itself. Leadership of an IEP team was also not in the equation; it never entered anyone's mind. Everyone knew that the outcome would be an individual education program (IEP), so what's the big deal. Well, it is a big deal, and I had to learn much in order to build the IEP teams that really made a difference not only in developing an IEP, but also increasing the probability of student success and achievement.

I have had the opportunity to look at this vehicle we call the IEP in three very different viewpoints. As an administrator I chaired hundreds of IEP team meetings, some excellent, some disappointing. As an elected school board member I saw the administrative costs, time, and resources dedicated to IEP team meetings and the necessity of rule compliance. However, my greatest experience was as a parent sitting on the other side of the table, seeing the IEP team meeting from a totally different perspective; that of the education and the future life of my own child.

These viewpoints gave me a dimension of really understanding what the IEP was meant to be and how the IEP team influenced every aspect of the special education student's education—before the meeting and after. I actualized the intent of the federal requirements while understanding the impact this group of people had on the quality of life for receivers of services from the outcome of the team-directed education plan.

This realization made a significant difference in the way I saw the outcome of the IEP as well as the manner in which the IEP team was led. It was not just a group of persons anymore; it was a vision of hope and the definition of the future. I finally saw the IEP as the vehicle to drive toward adulthood with success and dignity.

However, the vehicle could only go as far as the team of parents, student, and school staff could take it, under the direction of the person leading the initiative. Leading the IEP team made the most significant impact on the resulting IEP. IEP teams can look very similar; team capacities do not.

This writing was constructed for those who are learning to and for those who do lead IEP teams during and outside of the IEP team meeting. Following the steps and recommendations of this writing is not necessarily easy, but the methods are necessary for outstanding IEP teams, IEPs, and improving optimum potential of student success.

The primary premise is that you will need to treat every IEP like it is the most important meeting you have ever attended. Obviously the reader will be attending and chairing hundreds of IEP team meetings in a career. They will all seem to be cut from the same block of wood.

This book will help the leader and the entire IEP team to realize that IEP meetings are not all the same and that outstanding IEPs come from the leadership to build great IEP teams. The reader and all team members must realize that for the student, the IEP team meeting is the most important educational planning session that ever existed. The leader will need to create this culture within each IEP team, the school, and the district.

Putting ideas down and writing this book was difficult for a number of reasons. The most prominent is that while there is one special education law, one style for legally correct IEPs and related documentation, and one format is used by a school district, IEPs are different based upon the unique characteristics and the educational classification of each student.

Providing examples and detailed descriptors of how to report evaluation results, or determine supplemental aids and supports, will vary greatly between disability categories. The context of this writing was to promote concepts and ideas, not specifically related examples for all possible situations.

The concepts and ideas will help the leader translate actions relative to the individual situations of each student. While examples are provided, we all need to recognize that there is really no boilerplate for execution of the IEP team and IEP team meeting across all disability groups. This is why it is called an individual education program!

The writing does not address team functions of determining educational eligibility or educational placement. This writing is centered on team leadership functions and the development of the IEP, program reviews, and monitoring of progress. This is where most IEP team focus is directed and where IEP teams operate most of the time.

IEP team decisions regarding eligibility and educational placement are very important and should follow most of the material in this writing. However, these events usually take a perceived backseat to the actual education service plan.

ELIGIBILITY

Assessing a student's eligibility for special education services can be both an emotional and difficult decision, and at times the decision is very clear. There are problems with eligibility and there are often conflicts between school and parents—especially when parents have sought out-of-school recommendations and opinions.

These problems fall into two categories: (a) educational criteria for special education classification are different from those found in medical and psychological use, and (b) there are many mental health and medical issues diagnosable in a doctor's or psychologist's office that are not defined by the Individuals with Disabilities Education Act's (IDEA) definition for use by schools.

When there is a discrepancy between a medical or psychological diagnosis and one that is used in education, parents, doctors, and other licensed diagnosticians become instantly confused. Autism is a good example. The conditions defined in IDEA are different from the characteristics identified in the Diagnostic and Statistical Manual (DSM-IV TR). A parent may take their child to the pediatrician, who may suggest an autism spectrum disorder and ask for further assessments by persons trained in autism.

Using the DSM for guidance, the medical or psychological diagnostician may agree that the child has a spectrum disorder. However, when working with the school, the conditions and educational discrepancies for identification are not met and the child may not be eligible for special services or may be identified in a different special education classification. The same situation can exist for children with specific learning disabilities, emotional/behavioral disorders, and visual and hearing impairments.

Mental health issues are another area of concern. IDEA does not really address mental health. Often the IEP team is left to use an emotional/behavioral disorder or other health impairment to qualify students for special education services when the mental health issues interfere with the educational process.

Students with attachment issues, psychiatric impairments, and episodic deregulation are basically not included in the services that were designed to allow all students to find and benefit from special education and the benefits of a free and appropriate public education.

It is clear to the author that the federal and subsequent state laws relating to special education need to be shaped around the accepted DSM definitions of disability diagnosis. Besides confusing, it is disingenuous to say that in one environment such conditions exist and in other environments the disability does not exist.

Chronic and episodic mental health issues must be addressed by educators as a disability group to afford students the same successful educational opportunities to have their individual and unique needs met as do all other students.

Across the country there is, and have been, efforts made to effectively work with students with mental health concerns. However, there is not a model of best practice or even universal of promising educational methods. Educators must find successful models from other school districts and replicate such models in all districts in the country, similar to the manner in which special education services were nationally mandated in 1975.

EDUCATIONAL PLACEMENT

Where students with disabilities receive special education services is another major decision to be made by the IEP team. While there has been generalized movement since 1975 to provide inclusive education for all students, not all students with special needs actually receive education in regular education classes. Likewise there continues to be a movement to refrain from "pull-outs." There are no rules here, just the recommendations and decisions made by the student's IEP team.

Research and common practice demonstrate that inclusion for most students receiving special education is best, not only for the student with disabilities but also the "regular students." However, as much as we try to totally include all students, there will be a small percentage of children that require support and resources beyond the scope of what can be provided in a "regular" classroom. This is where decisions become difficult.

Everyone knows it is best practice and also politically correct to say all students with disabilities are taught in inclusive classes. However, for some students the degrees of accommodations and support necessary to assist the child with a severe disability may be problematic in an inclusive environment. Through response to intervention procedures and differentiated instruction, the outward appearance of heavy student supports may be made less obvious.

However, finding a way not to isolate the student with many direct supports in an integrated classroom will require leadership and a facilitative school culture. Leaders of the IEP will need to guide the team effectively through this process and make a decision during a fully constituted IEP team meeting.

Likewise, specialty services such as speech and occupational therapy may require "pull-out" sessions in order for these disciplines (bodies of knowledge) to deliver appropriate services. The degree of pull-outs and when the pull-outs occur are tricky questions, and again the team will need to determine the best time for each student.

Dealing with questions, discussion, and recommendations resulting in educational decisions cannot be based solely on what is in vogue, politically correct, or fits into the most commonly accepted philosophies. Decisions affecting young persons need to be based on the identified needs and preferred outcomes for the student expressed by the student, student's parents, and school professionals. This is why leadership, and as discussed later, transformational leadership, is necessary.

When transformational leadership guides and directs IEP team actions and behaviors to clearly focus on student needs and outcomes, then teams can effectively manage difficult issues and challenges. It accomplishes little if a school culture and poor chairing of an IEP team meeting produce unsatisfactory means to support students. These students will find little success, lose motivation, and see diminishing hope for the future.

The IEP team is important to the student, to the school staff, and to parents and is a reflection of the school district. Eligibility, placement, development of an IEP, monitoring, and reviewing progress are the basic team responsibilities. But the basic responsibilities go far beyond performing these duties.

The team has to enter into its responsibilities understanding what outcomes are expressed by each member of the team to ensure success in school, at home, and in the community. The team's primary responsibility is to pave a successful path to adulthood. That's it; and it starts and continues with the collaborative and productive IEP team meeting.

USING THIS BOOK

This book provides a general framework for the reader to become a leader; to lead meaningful and purposeful IEP teams. While learning how to lead teams, this framework also leads an effort to promote and build a positive understanding toward the IEP and the team meeting process. The culture transcends the school into acceptance, understanding, and a willingness to reach out to every student and their parents in respectful ways. The goal, of course, is student achievement leading to successful adult life.

Providing a general format such as is found in this writing means that the reader will need to make some adaptations to fit unique individual needs and situations of students and teams in the reader's school. While some examples are provided, these examples are only for the reader to expand conceptual knowledge to apply to individual student needs and support student outcomes.

The reader's aim is to fit the unique needs presented for each student, and his or her IEP team, into the scope of the IEP. While it is impossible for this writing to expound for every possible case, the ideas and concepts will help the reader act and think in different and collaborative ways. This is leadership; leadership that transforms team actions. This is what will drive the team toward outstanding IEPs and unrealized student success.

It is suggested that the reader read the short chapters one at a time and then review the analysis and the evaluation sections that are included in chapters 1 through 19. This effort will allow the reader to grasp the concepts and the implied school culture of the chapter to apply to individual situations.

Examples are used in cases when it may be beneficial for the reader to think differently about the topic in each chapter, but not necessarily to give the reader an exact dialogue for every situation faced as a team leader.

This work is outwardly compliant with IDEA, but more so, this work is based upon the spirit (soul) of the law. There is a difference, and it is "the spirit" of the law that propels the collaborative and cooperative leadership of the IEP team to do its work.

The IEP team can do this work effectively and efficiently following the spirit of the law. This spirit will extend new possibilities and expectations to ensure student achievement and application of skills in naturally occurring events and activities.

At different times in this writing, the author refers to a "pay now or pay more later" metaphor. This was taken from an old oil-filter television commercial that meant that if you pay a little up front to keep your car in top running shape, you will not need to pay a whole lot later when the car is running poorly. The thesis was, if the auto regularly uses this specific brand oil filter in the engine before the trouble starts, more expensive engine problems will not be present in the future.

This works for much of the theme of this writing. Doing some work ahead of the IEP team meeting will solve many of the much more difficult problems that could, and often do, occur after the team meeting.

While the work will appear at first overwhelming, hard, and time consuming, the reader begins to lead in "a culture of spirit" and collaboration. This system of leadership will passively influence the schools', students', and parents' attitude toward the IEP, and the results will progressively become easier and much more productive. To facilitate the reader's journey through this writing, the author has broken the book into three distinct yet integrated parts.

Part I will focus on building the IEP team to have greater balance, collaboration, and overall effectiveness. Part II is designed on the leadership required to transform the IEP team meeting to really meet individual students' needs in a collaborative environment. Part III studies the actual transformation of the team to become a great IEP team producing great IEPs.

IEP team meetings should be engaging, encouraging, and exciting. Following the framework of the spirit of IDEA removes the tedium, repetition, and compliance nature of the way you used to chair the IEP team meeting.

Kirby Lentz

Acknowledgments

Foremost, I deeply appreciate the opportunity of having a forty-year career working with students having intellectual disabilities, emotional/behavior disorders, autism, OHI disabilities, and a wide variety of low-frequency disabilities. I remember many and I will always remain impressed upon the degree to which each worked to learn, strive, and enjoy independence and contributions to our one society.

I was not sure this project would work, and without the prompting and ideas from my wife, BJ, this writing would be another undone "good idea that maybe would have been something." Hopefully this effort is something that will lead to a better life for a student in a school district and as an adult. BJ showed me in real life and in real time how to persevere, to keep going, and not give in to little and monster problems and tribulations.

I am indebted to the time and expertise of John Burnett, retired superintendent of Onalaska (WI) Public Schools; John Sachs, professor of special education, Southern Alabama University; Betty DeBoer, assistant professor of school psychology of the University of Wisconsin, La Crosse; and Sue Batell, dean; Bernie Ferry and Jim Bagneiski, associate professors of education at the Viterbo University. Their comments, insights, and recommendations to improve this writing are deeply appreciated and very necessary.

Finally and most important to the reader, my sincere appreciation to Dr. Tom Koerner, vice president and editorial director of Rowman & Littlefield Education, who saw the possibilities of this topic and offered much-needed and carefully considered thoughts and ideas to improve the topic and readability. The work would not have been possible without the help of assistant editor Carlie Wall and production editor Elaine McGarraugh.

I

BUILDING THE IEP TEAM

INTRODUCTION

Part I is a brief presentation of background information that is important for persons who chair IEP team meetings and those administrators and teachers who wish to improve the delivery of special education services. This part is a combination of proven business and organizational practices that are well documented in organizational development communities with new ideas about educational practices that are necessary to understand to move good IEP teams and good IEPs to great teams and IEPs.

Several organizational development theories and strategies are introduced in part I. These include the five disciplines of a learning organization (Senge), SWOT analysis (Humphrey), and transformational leadership (Burns). These ideas are critical to understanding how organizations such as an IEP team, a school building, or even an entire school district make education service improvement.

Improvement is without question the primary function to ensure that students with disabilities are afforded great teams and subsequently great IEPs. Great teams and great IEPs drive service delivery and educational services to make a meaningful pathway for students to follow toward a successful adulthood.

In this part, organization means all or any part of a local school district, such as an individual IEP team (the focus of this writing), but it can also be a school or district. The part of the organization that is projected to be affected by organizational change is referred to as the change unit, and again the change unit can be an IEP team, school, or district.

Many times when the change unit is small, such as an IEP team, the ramifications and outcomes of the change unit spread outwardly and overtly to the larger organization. This is the secondary goal of this book; however, student achievement and student use of functional life skills remain the most prominent initiatives of this writing.

Some educators not familiar with organizational development may feel confused by the short descriptions of strategies such as SWOT analysis, learning organizations, or transformational leadership. Appendix A will provide the author's impression of how these terms and techniques apply to an education environment; the reader may find it beneficial to go to the back of this book to get a more detailed and descriptive look at these terms.

Part I is perhaps more theoretical than practical, and this part should not flavor the very practical nature of part II. However, as in most efforts to introduce practice and common use, understanding some theory presents a background necessary to conceptualize and to justify practice. This is the case in part I.

Chapter 1 begins to introduce the leadership attributes necessary to gain great IEPs and IEP teams. The transformational leader will be introduced as well as perhaps some familiar traits of persons chairing IEP team meetings.

Chapter 2 explains the learning environments for students with disabilities, not just in the classroom or the school building. Environments for learning outside of the school building perhaps offer the greatest opportunities for learning.

Chapter 3 introduces the efforts required to build positive and collaborative relationships between parent and teacher, home and school. Great IEP teams have honest and fully participating teams. These teams come from respectful and responsible relations of all team members.

Chapter 4 explains a new theory of why teams miss all kinds of opportunities to provide great IEPs and develop great IEP teams. This chapter will set the stage for the very practical aspects of leadership of the IEP team in part II.

As a community, education must be able to look at business strategies and organizational theory with open eyes and minds. Obviously not all techniques found in business apply to education. Most educators have heard the true story of the "ice cream man in Iowa who made the best ice cream in the country." If not, ask someone to tell you this fascinating story. However, organization development has made significant headway into the ways an organization or change unit can think about total quality management, or simply organizational effectiveness.

Improvement is critical in education, far beyond the implications of federal accountability found in No Child Left Behind and a variety of state reports demonstrating special education progress. Accountability is necessary for our local neighbors and taxpayers. In the absence of reputable and verifiable methods to exhibit what the public considers as progress, educators need to find authentic ways to say that what is done in special education is really being good for all students.

Great IEPs and great IEP teams will lend toward such authenticity of progress and justification for the resources that go into local educational systems, and into special education. Educators need to be very concerned about how, today and in the future, the public, state, and federal departments of education view, and assess the value and worth, of education. Part I will lay out an introduction to just that.

1

The People on the Team

KEY POINTS

1. The style of the leader or chair of the IEP team meeting can and will influence the outcome of the team meeting, affecting student potential.
2. The leadership style of the team meeting can be one that lasts for the school life of the student.
3. The leader is one who designs, teaches, and helps others to do their best.

If one were asked to paint a picture of the IEP team meeting in action, there would be a multitude of themes, scenes, and expressions. Perhaps the picture would include a round table, persons looking friendly, someone talking, others listening, organized papers in front of each individual. There may be someone writing and someone even printing ideas on a whiteboard in an attractive room at school. A student, parents, and a variety of teachers and specialists would look engaged, happy, and interested.

Perhaps the picture would look very different. The room may be the same as in the previous painting, but the persons around the table would be painted to look unhappy, bored, or even angry. There would be no individual using the whiteboard or taking notes, and the attendees do not look to be engaged or interested. There could be hundreds of different scenes painted to describe what IEP team meetings look like.

All IEP team meetings should look like the first scene, and most readers will easily recognize this. This type of meeting does not just happen. Meetings like this are developed over time and are constructed by a transformational leader of the IEP team. A transformational leader is one who is committed to the individual outcomes of every student receiving special education services.

It is this person who understands both the letter and the spirit of the Individuals with Disabilities Education Act (IDEA) or the special education law, sees and believes in the potential of every student. The transformational leader projects an actualization of the district's potential to exceed expected service delivery to every district student. It takes leadership and a transformational leader to paint this picture.

The transformational leader is one who has developed the engagement of students, parents, and school staff involved in the IEP process. Everyone knows what and who each IEP attendee is and the roles each will play in the team meeting. The transformational leader in this picture expects that everyone attending is prepared, has completed all necessary work such as assessments and summaries, and has ensured that all participants are comfortable participating in the meeting discussions.

The leader, including the student and leading the meeting with supports from parents for the transformational leader, will chair the meeting. But in addition the leader has worked with team members before the meeting to ensure that they are prepared and follows up with members after the meeting to monitor implementation and assessment of individual programs. The actual chairing of the IEP meeting is just a part of the job of the leader who sees the entire IEP process as a system providing differentiated services to meet identified needs of students.

The other pictures that are sometimes painted of IEP team meetings tend to be painted by teams without a transformational leader, or a leader at all. A "chairperson" is not always a leader. Instead of a transformational leader, these teams have a "Git-'er done person" who will chair the IEP meeting. The Git-'er done chairperson is not bad, unfriendly, or uncaring. The Git-'er-done just wants to get the IEP team done and over, usually without much regard for its content and potential outcomes for the student.

The Git-'er done person does not understand the full nature of the IEP team responsibilities. The Git-'er done person does not see the relationship of team leadership to team outcomes. The Git-'er done runs the IEP meeting and gets it done and that's it. Pretty simple and very straightforward: the Git-'er done leaves few leadership qualities or impressions on the members of the team, the school culture, or team effectiveness.

The success and the failure of the IEP team to develop great IEPs are directly related to the style of the team leader. Therefore, this chapter is about the concept of defining the leadership of the IEP team, how this leadership affects the persons on the team, and the methods the team chair utilizes before, after, and during the IEP team meeting. Leadership is then responsible for the success of the student's IEP and success transitioning toward adult living.

THE TEAM

IDEA specifically defines who is a member of a student's IEP team, who must attend team meetings, and with some procedural work which team members can be excused from the meeting. IDEA clearly wants to ensure that all areas of the student's educational life are included in the meetings and efforts to direct education to prepare the student for adulthood successfully. The law (IDEA) also desires for this group of persons to each have an equal role and level of participation in the IEP team meeting.

The team members are identified to the parents when the Notice of an IEP Team Meeting form is sent to parents from the school in advance of the team meeting. This notice also identifies the titles and the assumed roles of each identified member who will attend the team meeting. The purpose of this notice and the identification of members is to allow the parents to see who will attend and what position each attendee has. While the invited members of the student's IEP team under the special education law is fairly clear, the nature of the roles and the impact of the team's leader is not clear and often misunderstood by team members.

So why then is a chapter dedicated to the persons on the IEP team? The answer is rather simple; it's not the title or role of the team member that is important, but it is the style and type of leadership made available to the persons on the IEP team. Educators know, for example, that IDEA requires a regular education teacher; a special education teacher certified in the student's disability; appropriate related service personnel, such as a speech and language pathologist when there is an identified speech and language need present; an occupational or physical therapist for any fine or gross motor concerns; an administrator; the student; and the student's parents or guardians. IDEA also allows for others to participate, including a third-party facilitator, a parent advocate, attorneys for school and parents, and parent-school liaisons.

IDEA, however, does not define or prescribe the leadership style and team relationships. While it is important that all team members clearly understand the boundaries and expertise of each member, members must also be conscious of the limits, expectations, and knowledge of professional and parental areas of responsibility.

There are, however, few boundaries or limits placed on the IEP team leader by IDEA and rarely in district policy or practice. The role of leadership is essential but has received little attention from the law, in practice, and from the literature.

How the IEP team and the IEP meeting are led becomes an important topic to understand. Leadership defines how IEP teams behave. Leaders of the team influence the way in which team members interact, how the IEP is developed and implemented, and the manner in which members coordinate and work together. The leader is usually a school staff member (although parents and students have, should, and can lead the IEP team meeting well; see more in chapter 9). The leader takes the team through some fashion of an agenda. The leader's goal in the IEP team meeting depends upon the style of the leader.

For purposes of this writing, there are two general styles of being in charge of the IEP team meeting: (a) the Git-'er done chairperson, whose goal is to get to the end of the meeting because that is where the Git-'er done person sees the termination of responsibilities; and (b) the person employing the principles and qualities of transformational leadership.

For example, the transformational leader who is committed to leadership qualities will see the goal of the team, respectfully look at every possible opportunity, and move the team toward an educational outcome that is built strongly around student needs within the context of input from every member of the team.

Each IEP team needs a transformational leader who is committed to a belief in individual student achievement. A leader is one who sees the IEP team meeting as a specific and ongoing planning meeting—one in which participants are prepared, the team knows what its job is, the members are equally engaged, and the end of the meeting is really the beginning of actions agreed upon by the entire IEP team. A Git-'er done person does not do this. It takes transformational leadership to guide the IEP team to a destination of functional student achievement and success.

The great IEP is a long-term team effort, and it will involve a series of IEP team meetings over several school years and with a variety of team leaders and team members. For example, when the student moves from elementary to middle school, an entirely new set of team chairs and staff members come into play. Good transitions begin with and are maintained by good leadership. To understand more fully how an IEP team leader influences what the IEP team does, we will need to look at some general types of IEP team leaders.

THE GIT-'ER DONE TYPES

The Git-'er done person who is assigned to chair a particular IEP team meeting is one who will do *just* that; this person lets anyone who wants to make their statements do so whenever they wish. Or if members do not try hard to be heard, their information will not be shared; the team or the chair will garner just enough information to formulate a couple of goals, will quickly

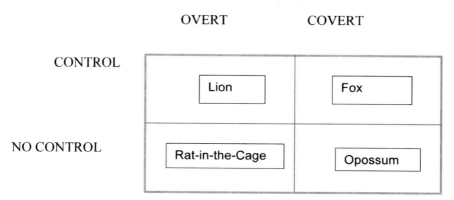

Figure 1.1. Git-'er Done chairperson characteristics.

review the related services, skim the supplemental supports stuff, and adjourn the meeting.

While this is a basic premise of the IEP Git-'er done chair, the Git-'er can take on one of four styles: the Lion, the Fox, the Opossum, and the Rat-in-the-Cage (see figure 1.1). Most Git-'er done chairs of IEP teams will fall into one of these patterns. The style of the Git-'er done persons fails to build team capacity and can severely influence and negatively impact the outcomes of the IEP. The IEP of this style of team meeting will most likely fail any efforts for future student success and achievement.

The Lion (Overt Control Master)

The Lion roars his or her way through the IEP team meeting agenda, literally using the special education law, district policy, and school procedures to the absolute letter. To support this overt control of the IEP process, the Lion will not deviate from the expected and planned route that the Lion sets for the operation of the team even if the route makes no sense to the outcomes and purpose of the meeting.

What happens at one IEP team meeting happens at another. This is the way the Lion proceeds, and don't let anyone get in the way. The Lion does not like questions or new ideas, because there is little room on the preconceived plan for interruption or deviation from the planned agenda. The Lion does things in this way because the law says it is done this way, even when other ideas make sense for the student.

The Lion is free to refer to the explicit letter of the special education law because the Lion needs to complete the task as the Lion sees it, especially on any tricky situation. For example, in a disagreement of extended school year (ESY) or summer school between the school psychologist, the parent, and the Lion, the Lion will interject that the law states that there needs to be justifiable and statistically verifiable regression of academic skills to support ESY and there is not enough evidence that regression will statistically occur without ESY; case closed and move on!

The Lion is unbending. The Lion is dogmatic and utilizes strict interpretation of IDEA, school policy, or practices used in the district. The Lion will use the law, policy, and procedure as necessary to beef up the Lion's style of operation, to support the Lion's need to reach meeting adjournment; not necessarily to construct a great IEP or reach consensus, or even have discussions on important student issues.

Characteristics of the Lion include procedural blinders, following the letter of the law when it fits the Lion's ideas, and aggressively and literally interpreting the law as viewed from the Lion's perspective. If the law is not clear to support the Lion's perspective, the Lion will have little regard for input, information, or ideas from others and expect little to no deviation from a rigid agenda.

The Lion will usually have the goals of the IEP team meeting prepared or even in place before the meeting begins, even though the special education law prohibits this—they just magically appear. The agenda the Lion will impose at the team meeting will be directly aimed at these predetermined conclusions and etches a pathway for the team to move in unison directly toward this end.

The Lion's IEP style of the IEP meeting is management, not leadership, and the goal is to get to adjournment as soon as possible. Efforts are made to minimally cover all required topics in as little depth as can be. Depth of the meeting can be defined as reaching the outcomes set by the Lion ahead of the meeting, and all discussions and actions are directed toward these outcomes. Deviations from these predetermined outcomes equal increased time in the meeting. The Lion's perception of contribution to the environment is the Lion will save everyone time and uphold the special education law in its strictest sense. There is no confusion!

The Fox (Covert Control Master)

The Fox is also a rule user, but unlike the Lion, the Fox is cunning in its attempt to get through the team meeting agenda. The Fox, like the Lion, usually has developed the end product before the meeting and will direct the agenda to get to these predetermined results. The Fox, however, will do this in manipulative ways.

Where the Lion goes straight to the point, the Fox will be sly about its behavior to gain its goal. For example, the Fox will set the meeting flavor by asking scripted school staff to report first in order to set the stage for the Fox's agenda and preferred outcome, or will thank parents or students for their thought-out input but clearly forget about this information when either summarizing the meeting or constructing the IEP.

In other cases the Fox will control parent and student participation by breaking up conversations and pointing out that "the Law" will not allow or permit certain key issues made by parents and even others on the team. The Law rules, and this is played out often in underlying and manipulative ways to benefit the interests of the Fox.

The Fox, unlike the Lion, does not have a set agenda, but the Fox will bounce from topic to topic depending upon the flavor of the meeting and the Fox's need to keep the discussion moving toward the Fox's outcome for the meeting—an easy conclusion.

The operation of the Fox is mired in IDEA, and the Fox's interpretation of the Law therefore allows the Fox to manipulate to acquire predetermined and prescribed outcomes. Like the Lion, the Fox likes to get the job done without much need to accept other input. But unlike the Lion, the Fox tries to be perceived as supportive to all team members, yet underneath manipulates the approach, discussion, and outcomes.

The Lion will bully through the agenda; the Fox will cunningly manipulate through the meeting. For example, the Fox will redirect a conclusion previously made by a school staff member when input or a request is made by the student, parent, or another school representative. This will be done nicely, but with the intent of demonstrating that this has already been discussed and the idea is really not very good.

When the Fox is successful in casting a net of doubt over disagreeing school staff, students, or parents, the Fox has gained tight control of the meeting and the meeting agenda and proceeds with the preconceived agenda and outcomes without coming across as dictating to or controlling of the team function.

The style of the Fox is similar to the Lion, but less obvious. The Fox will try to be the "nice guy" while massaging the Fox's predetermined agenda and outcomes. Many participants feel they were engaged in a productive team meeting but have a sense of "something was funny" about the meeting, especially perceived by students and parents.

Like the Lion, the Fox's contribution is to save time and use the letter of "the Law." Unlike the Lion, the Fox will not cause uproar or anything different from the perceived outcome of the meeting, manipulating the team to agreement and thinking the team did the IEP, not the Fox.

The Opossum (No Control and Covert)

The Opossum attempts to get through the meeting without conflict, disruption, or making decisions on difficult or demanding situations. The Opossum will likely keep a meeting going and going to avoid having to make a difficult decision, or to hope that a team member will make a recommendation to end the discussion. The Opossum is very good at looking dead, especially during contentious times experienced in some IEP team meetings. Yet the Opossum offers just enough life to let team members know the chairperson is not total roadkill.

The Opossum will keep the team meeting going until the time in which other team members solve some of the major issues. Often this is the time the Opossum will then awaken and request that the team take a break or stop at this point and reconvene at a later time. The Opossum manages the team by using all efforts to avoid conflict and to avoid being put in a decision-making position.

The Opossum falsely says the role of team chair is one that keeps everything on the table and alive in the discussion. In other words, do not ask the Opossum to summarize, offer an opinion, or make a recommendation to bring topics to a close. The Opossum really is uncomfortable in the role of chairperson but tries to hide this with an overarching smile and statements such as, "Say whatever you want. Everything you say is important to the team; we will consider all of your input."

Saying this to parents, students, and school personnel is simply a way to have others talk and interact without the Opossum's involvement or taking a stand. The theme is, if everyone talks, the Opossum does not have to. The Opossum is noncommitted, does not use IDEA in any meaningful way, and will not cross any lines between fellow team members.

The Opossum's style is somewhat outside of the special education law, and the Opossum surprisingly does not refer to IDEA to clarify sticky points. The Opossum is most comfortable watching the team action going around the Opossum's comfort zone—often comfortable being half dead. The Opossum is in fear of having to make a decision, or a recommendation, or a commitment in which there may be disagreement.

The Opossum would rather, and usually does, play dead during times that leadership and direction should be presented. The Opossum is most grateful when the meeting has concluded and everyone has left—regardless of the team meeting's outcomes or educational impact for the student.

The characteristic of the Opossum is to never end the IEP team meeting until someone puts a decision on the table and the team accepts it. The Opossum would rather keep the team meeting going when conflicts arise than offer a remedy to the problematic issues.

The Opossum is rather favorable to follow-up meetings and will wait until other team members take the ownership of team decisions. The Opossum will justify actions (non-actions) by stating that the contribution of the Opossum is allowing all members to have a chance to participate; but the real contribution is everyone gets a lot of meeting time, too much time to realize any practical student outcomes.

The Rat-in-the-Cage (No Control and Overt)

The Rat-in-the-Cage simply does not want to be at the IEP team meeting. The Rat-in-the-Cage will let everyone know that the IEP team meeting is the Cage and IEP team meetings are just "dumb," that no matter what happens, nothing good comes from it. There is no purpose for the team meeting (Cage), and the Rat will spit and hiss at everyone coming near the Cage or wanting to participate in the team meeting.

The Rat does not want to chair the IEP team meeting, does not like the team members, and may even perceive that the members of the team put the Rat into the Cage. The Rat does not think the IEP process or special education even works, and everything surrounding the IEP, special education, and related services is just a waste of his and others' time; it does not make any difference at the end of the day!

The Rat-in-the-Cage expresses displeasure at most everything about the team meeting. The Rat will see little purpose of any discussion, because there will be nothing different after the discussion; there is little hope of any plans being successful because nothing ever happens and we are just wasting time.

The Rat's mantra is, "let's get through this stuff so we can go back and do our jobs." The Rat-in-the-Cage really does not care much about the team meeting; getting done and getting on are necessary goals without regard for any quality or innovation in the IEP or service delivery—nothing ever changes anyway, so why care.

The Rat-in-the-Cage's characteristics are clearly outside the letter and the spirit of the special education law and district policy and practice, and imply that the law is ridiculous and district policy is worthless. The Rat's principal operation is, "Let's just do what we did last time and get back to something important." The Rat's traits are usually hostile, angry, and nonproductive. Often the Rat-in-the-Cage is well known in the school district as ineffective, and the threat of change to the Rat does not change the style; there is often little consequence for not caring!

There is little concern about individual student needs and even less about student success in school. The Rat also does not want to chair the meeting and wants even less to be a leader. The Rat will express little regard for follow-ing the letter or the spirit of the special education law. Everything except the Rat's own job responsibilities—obviously chairing the IEP team meeting is not one of them—is not important and therefore really unnecessary.

The style of the Rat is to get the meeting started and then moan about it through the entire process. Since there are no gains from the team meeting, the Rat clearly makes no claim for any contributions. The meeting should be five minutes long, and it really does not matter what is said, discussed, or decided in these five minutes; Big Deal!

This generalized characterization of Git-'er done IEP chairpersons is why IEP team meetings often fail; the goal is to simply get to the end of the agenda. Git-'er doners do not accept this role as a leadership role, usually just as a mandate that interferes with their work life. Students with disabilities, their parents, and all the school personnel involved with IEP team meetings require and deserve to have great team leaders. Transformational leaders and professionals who can appreciate and demand grounded information, sharing of pertinent data, and equal engagement by all team members including the student and are able to look into the future to see potential and opportunities are the leaders IEP teams deserve and need; they transform great IEPs to actualizing student success.

TRANSFORMATIONAL LEADERSHIP STYLE

While the Lion, Fox, Opossum, and the Rat symbolize the negative styles of IEP leaders, a fifth style is the preferred: the transformational leadership style of the IEP team. Transformational leadership is a quality that positively motivates and moves good ideas forward. The styles seen in the Lion, Fox, Opossum, or Rat are concerned with manipulation, deceit, disengagement, and power. They are not leaders and generally do more damage by their selfishness and lack of caring than they manage to achieve in any facet of the IEP process. Transformational leadership is seen as the only style that *leads* the IEP team.

Peter Senge, author of *The Fifth Discipline* (1990), a business strategist known for developing *systems thinking* as a means to improve business or-ganizations, was once asked what leadership is. Senge stated that leadership consists of three characteristics seen from transformational leaders: they are designers, teachers, and servants. This is what our school staff, parents, and students should have and are asking for to lead the student's IEP team meet-ing. This is the major difference between transformational leadership and just chairing or applying Git-'er done style to the IEP team meeting.

When transformational leadership is evidenced, the leader and the team naturally experience a process that lasts over time and creates exciting possibilities for individual students. The transformational leader sees all persons on the team as integral to this process, and input from all is required, important, and sought after in respectful ways.

The leader knows how to be a leader within the scope of the district's policies and resources; therefore, the leader seeks what is best for the student and is not one who grants every wish to parents or the district. Leadership is not a giver of things; leadership is getting teams to work together to solve student-driven situations using the three attributes Senge used to describe a leader: designing, teaching, and serving.

Designing of the IEP Team

The designer part of a leader is not that the person leading the team meeting designs the program; it means the leader designs the potential and the possibilities of the program, so the organization can be built the best it can be. Designing an agenda to meet the known needs of a student, designing a method to solicit reasonable and important outcomes, creating measurable goals from educational outcomes, developing a model for culture change, and enhancing organizational improvement are examples of designing.

School professionals often think that IDEA is the designer of special education services, or perhaps school policy defines what the delivery of special education is. It is important that the members of the student's team consider the law and policy as direction setting, but the actual design of the student's educational services is created by transformational leadership along with the team members.

Designing is tough because it is never a one-size-fits-all. The leader of the team must facilitate the team to build the service around the student, not only by enforcing district policy or previous practices.

When the IEP team leader is engaging the team in design, the leader has created both an environment that supports equality of membership and removal of all predetermined biases and negative beliefs and a safe place for discussion and idea sharing without fear of retribution or disregard.

The transformational leader has to create this environment, and this environment does not occur with the Git-'er done chairperson. Leadership is designing when it encompasses the service delivery process on a very individual basis; when the student and the team are valued and leadership respects all contributions to promote meaningful opportunities for student success.

Teaching of the IEP Team

A leader as the teacher, Senge's second attribute to leadership, is preparing the team to function together—to discuss, plan, and implement. To function and operate well, the leader will need to teach and train participants to know how to be great team members, what the expectations of a great team are, and how members actualize expectations within a team organization.

Teaching is an essential part of leadership. Leadership is preparing the members of the team to know what it is that the team can potentially optimize for each student. While it may seem natural to know what to do to be a team member, it is essential that the leader teach the team in certain aspects of the IEP team responsibilities. Teaching team members, including parents, students, and teachers, is discussed fully in chapter 12, but the conscientious leader will put serious importance on teaching for effectiveness.

When all members of the team have received training and have a clear idea of what is expected from oneself as well as others, the members can work in a safe, productive, and creative work environment. It is within this type of a setting that great work can be accomplished.

The author has seen tremendous results when teachers and parents were taught collaborative meeting initiatives even when previous meetings were heated and difficult. Teaching helps keep everyone on the same level playing field and helps all understand areas of expertise and involvement.

Serving Others on the IEP Team

Finally as a servant, Senge's third attribute of leadership, the leader does what any other member would be expected to do. As a team leader, the leader will help each individual member achieve their best. The leader sets the example: is on time, is prepared for the team meeting, is thought-out in ideas, and is capable of listening to others and then forming veritable conclusions and ideas from hearing input. The servant also helps others to do their job well and to improve.

The leader must be mentally positioned to learn what team members need. The leader must be able to provide the members with reasonable resources, supplies, time, information, and knowledge that are critical to the work members are engaged to do.

The author has experienced times when the IEP team leader helped cover a class so the specialist could have more time to work on a difficult evaluation, and a specialist helping another teacher after school attempting to formulate some ideas for the upcoming IEP team meeting. Servant leadership is serving others so that others may shine and demonstrate to others respect and affirmation.

Developing leadership takes commitment and dedication. The leader must be willing to learn how to best lead the student's IEP team and reach achievable, realistic, and purposeful educational success. Part II of this work will provide information on how leadership of the IEP occurs and is maintained. But the goal of this work is to reinforce that teams need leaders, leaders can be developed, and students deserve to have functioning teams that are built by professionals that design, teach, and serve—team leadership.

The Individuals with Disabilities Education Act defines the persons involved in the student's IEP team; the law does not define the attributes that members bring to the team, and neither does the law define by whom or how the team is led. So the persons on the team need to reflect upon their role and their understanding of their contribution to the overall effort.

The law is cumbersome and it is involved, but the spirit of the law is to ensure that all students, including those students with disabilities, are afforded an education service delivery that makes success possible. This success can only be achieved through the direction and manner in which the IEP and the IEP team function toward this end.

Leadership is critical. The team will function only as well as the leadership that is employed in real time. The next chapter will discuss the role of environments in which most students participate in life and how these environments interact within the function of the IEP team and the resulting IEP.

ANALYSIS

1. How does leadership affect student achievement?
2. Why are designing, teaching, and servant roles important to the function of the IEP team?
3. What are you going to do to incorporate transformational leadership at your next IEP team meeting?

EVALUATION

1. Are you a chair, or do you think you would be a chair of an IEP team meeting?
2. If so, are you a Lion, Fox, Opossum, or a Rat-in-the-Cage?
3. What steps are you going to make to become an IEP team leader?
4. Are you better suited to be a designer, teacher, or servant, or can you be all three at the same time?

5. Can you see things you can do to improve on having the attributes of a transformational leader where you feel you are not as strong as you think you should be?

6. What will you do differently next time you are in a leadership role for an IEP team meeting?

2

The Learning Environments

School, Home, and the Community

KEY POINTS

1. Student needs occur outside of the school curriculum and state standards.
2. Students participate in life within three environments: school, home, and the community.
3. The Test of Utility is a means to assess the use and purpose of what students with disabilities are asked to learn.

When educators think of where education services take place, most parents, students, teachers, and school staff will say in the classroom. Perhaps in some cases another location will be mentioned such as a resource room, the gym, or the speech therapy room, but it is most universally thought that education takes place at school. Furthermore, it is most commonly thought that what is taught in the classroom are the academics—the three Rs.

This is what most people think schools are for: to teach academic skills—a thought that has persisted for at least the past couple of centuries. Educators think that when children are learning in school they are learning academics; everything else that is learned mostly happens at home and in the community. However, this thought is confounded when one considers the education of and learning environment for students with disabilities and understands the spirit of the law.

Skills taught to students with disabilities at school often go beyond the concept of "pure" academics. Skills being taught and that educators are asking students to learn often in special education go outside of the academic paradigm. These skills, after the skill is learned, must be able to be used functionally in real living environments experienced by the student.

STUDENT NEEDS OUTSIDE OF SCHOOL

While consensus posits that academic skills are taught at school and every-thing else is taught at home; this thought is definitely not true for students with disabilities. The axiom is, if learning life skills is necessary for success-ful adult living, and if learned behaviors occur at home and at school, most of these skills must be taught both in school and at home; purely academic or not. This author has heard too many times, "We don't teach [blank] in school." The [blank] has included toileting, dressing, social skills, appropriate touching behaviors, bullying, physical skills such as balancing, food stealing, materials stealing, property and materials destruction, running away from assigned areas or even the school campus, sensory diets and sensory integra-tion, relationship skills, appropriate social behaviors, and this is only a start.

IEP teams need to understand that prevailing issues presented by the student need to be addressed. Since most prevailing issues are not limited to environmental boundaries, these issues will usually be seen across three environments: school, home, and the community.

While it is true that children (and adults) behave differently in different environments, many students with disabilities cannot make the connection of one set of behaviors for one environment, another set of behaviors in another environment.

For example, the author remembers a young boy who loved to go to the basketball games and yelled with everyone else when the home team was in-troduced to the fans before beginning play. This was an appropriate behavior for the environment in which the behavior was displayed. However, when the same young boy attended the school play and when the first actor stepped on stage, this was not the time for the same wild and boisterous cheer and yell that was so appropriate at the basketball game.

Toileting is not an academic skill; it is a prevailing issue because toileting issues can occur at school. This makes toileting an issue to be addressed at school. The same goes for stealing, destruction of property, running away, and inappropriate touching as examples. It becomes a school issue when it happens at school, even when thought to be a home issue.

Teachers of students with disabilities would like to see skills learned at school reinforced at home and in the community. Parents in the same way need to have the school staff assist in the "not academic," yet important life skills necessary to be learned by the student. In the author's experience, toileting is usually the biggest issue—no one really likes to deal with it. But it happens—at home, in the community, and at school. It has to be dealt with effectively.

Chapter 10 in part II will explain how learning is developed across a multitude of environments. The goal of IEPs is to ensure that students with disabilities learn lifelong independent skills. Well, toileting is one of them. Parents will hear from school staff, "Toileting does not fit with any of the state standards and we can only have goals that are directly aligned to state standards, so toileting does not fit." This is the work of the Git-'er done person discussed in the previous chapter.

The transformational leader will understand the state standard thing and immediately go to a very important part of the IEP agenda: supplemental aids and supports. This is the area where important lifelong skills as well as individually focused supports, such as toilet training, are usually and effectively addressed.

In this case a simple toileting schedule can be structured into the student's schedule, ideas for toileting strategies may be referred to an occupational therapist for program evaluation or one of several toilet training methodologies available to be implemented. The points are (a) if it happens at school it must be addressed at school and (b) if it is important to the student with disabilities it needs to be part of the IEP, as either a goal or a supplemental aid and support.

There is also a legitimate concern for home–school interventions when behaviors are presented differently in school and at home. Recently there has been concern with children having significant attachment issues. The child will engage in a variety of serious attachment-related behaviors at home and with parents and guardians in the community. However, at school the student presents as sweet and charming. Because the school does not see any aberrant behaviors, the school's position is "not here—no problem." This has led to confusion, disagreement, and anger from parents and guardians who are attempting to deal with severely interfering behaviors and seemingly no concern from the school.

The advice of professionals needs to be sought and considered, and even though behaviors are not overtly displayed at school, if there are recommendations by experts to deal with a lifelong behavior pattern, any assistance by the school can be addressed in the supplemental aids and supports section of the agenda and the IEP.

THE SCHOOL IS A CONTRIVED ENVIRONMENT

It is hoped in school that all learning will lead to the functional use of the learned skills in life to either make life more functional or to improve the quality of life. However, most curricular topics taught in school are presented in an environment that is not real.

When teachers teach fractions, they pretend they have a pizza and ask the students, "If there are eight slices of pizza, and you have four friends, how many slices of pizza will each friend get to eat so that all friends will have a quarter (1/4) of the pizza and the same amount for each friend?" A student will yell, "Two!" Then the teacher will show how two is 1/4 of the whole pizza.

The teacher does not teach this skill so when the rare time comes that the student has three other friends over at his house and there is one pizza cut into eighths, the student will know that each one will get two slices or each will have 1/4 of the pizza. The teacher tries to make the fraction example applicable and interesting, but it does not occur in a natural or real environment.

Most regular education students are able to understand that the learning environment is not real and are able to make adjustments to understand and separate the concept and the application. But for many students with disabilities, taking a skill learned in a contrived environment and applying this same learned skill in a real environment would be difficult and perhaps not even possible.

For example, in the classroom, a boy with cognitive disabilities is learning to add single-digit numbers on a worksheet given to him by his teacher. On the worksheet are several problems, all requiring single-digit addition, such as:

$$
\begin{array}{cccc}
2 & 5 & 3 & 1 \\
+2 & +1 & +4 & +7 \\
\hline
=\rule{1cm}{0.4pt} & =\rule{1cm}{0.4pt} & =\rule{1cm}{0.4pt} & =\rule{1cm}{0.4pt}
\end{array}
$$

Without regard to the methodology used to instruct single-digit addition, touch math, memorization, or finger counting, the use of this skill can be applied only to this worksheet and perhaps a rote recall if asked, "What is two plus two?" There will be little, if any, utilization in the real world.

What would happen to this little boy if he was learning to add single-digit numbers at school, not with worksheets but with real objects such as items in his lunch box, when he goes home and his mother asks him to help set the table for dinner, saying, "We need two plates for you and your sister, and two plates for Dad and me; how many plates do I need to put on the counter for you to take to the table?"

When home and school are able to work together, and when the contrived learning environment at school and the real environment at home and in the community can work together, utilization becomes purposeful and learning is reinforced.

TEACHING SKILLS IN MULTIPLE ENVIRONMENTS

The aforementioned example of adding single-digit numbers in school and at home is an example of teaching in multiple environments. Such teaching is very effective, especially for the student with disabilities, because the student is able to experience some use of the skill in naturally occurring events and in real time. The learning process is naturally reinforced.

Adding two-digit numbers becomes not just a futile exercise on a meaningless sheet of paper, but becomes alive when the skill is applied at home and in the community. Then the student experiences utility and purpose of the learning skill; a veritable existence of education!

School staff needs to understand that children live in three environments: school, home, and the community. Realizing that schools are contrived environments but the other environments of home and community are real is very important for teachers to remember. Educators need to keep the contrived nature of school in mind because much of the learning that students receive is in these contrived places.

When learning is presented formally and informally in a variety of natural environments in addition to the contrived environment of school, learning is reinforced because the student will have an understanding of how the skill can be used or should be used to improve the student's independence and quality of one's life. When application is understood by the student, then the skill receives greater student focus and attention.

TEST OF UTILITY

Educators often ask students to learn difficult and demanding subject material. Teachers know that many students work very hard to learn what is asked of them. Therefore, the materials those educators ask of students with disabilities to learn must be applicable and usable—to be utilized in the student's real life.

A simple Test of Utility is a good guide for educators to use: if the skill being instructed to the student can be used as a learned skill outside of the classroom in a natural environment then the skill should be taught along with instructions of how to use the learned skill and why in the real world.

If the learned skill will not be part of the student's repertoire of utilized acquired skills, the effort of and time from the student for learning should not be expected: the skill should not be taught. For example, teaching a child to do long division by hand and as a paper-and-pencil activity will not stand up to the Test of Utility. The Test of Utility would demonstrate that long division is completed with a hand calculator.

Teaching a student to use a hand calculator to complete a long division problem and how to apply long division in the student's life would satisfy the Test of Utility. The author freely admits that he will look longer to find a calculator to figure out a long division problem than it would take to use paper and pencil and actually figure out what he needed to know.

This test will probably kill half of the state standards mandated for our nation's school districts, but the test is incontrovertible. The teacher and the IEP team need to consider utility even within sight and threat of state standards and federal rules. Students with disabilities work hard to learn new skills, so the skills educators ask students to learn must be skills that are to be used at home and in the community, and as an adult.

THE IEP TEAM

The leadership qualities discussed in the previous chapter now become essential. The leader of the IEP team must be able to (a) lead the IEP team to design a program plan that works in multiple environments, (b) teach team members how to arrive at functional goals and utilitarian educational outcomes, (c) implement the necessary goals and support skills to ensure best possible opportunities for successful adult living, and (d) assist the IEP team to recognize overall need for education improvement through a collaborative IEP process.

When the team understands that learning occurs in the three environments of school, home, and community, the team is then ready to gather input from all IEP team members. The team will want to get and hear information about the outcomes teachers, parents, and students identify as important. A good way for teams to get such information is through the process described in chapter 12 of part II.

Through this process outcomes are developed by students and parents using a format that includes an assessment of learned and emerging skills, aligning emerging skills to realistic outcomes, and understanding how outcomes relate to people in the student's life as described and assessed by students and parents. This information is presented to the IEP team as part of a parent and a student assessment and used to create and design an educational program that can be incorporated into all three environments in the student's life.

While it is true the IEP team must follow the laws of the state and the federal rules that apply to delivery of special education services, the IEP must also provide student utility and purpose for the student. When the leader of the IEP team, and subsequently the IEP team, can design an educational program that is realistic and functional so that learned skills can be utilized in real and naturally occurring events and places, the IEP will serve its intended purpose and will prepare students for life success.

ANALYSIS

1. How does the contrived nature of education at schools and in classrooms affect the learning strategy for students with disabilities?
2. Why are the environments of home and community important to include within the plan for education services?
3. How will you apply the Test of Utility to assess the merits of the goals and other provisions of the developing student's IEP?

EVALUATION

1. Did the IEP team consider the home, school, and community environmental impacts at the last IEP team meeting?
2. Did the IEP team, or members of the team, refer to the Test of Utility for recommended action plans to be considered as part of the IEP?
3. What steps will you, as the IEP team leader, do to incorporate home, school, and community environments in planning program initiatives?
4. Does the IEP team understand the contrived nature of school and classroom?

.ioption.

n a relationship-b.

collaborative and

ns, and school.

as demonstra

vivement

3

Building Relationships

KEY POINTS

1. Creating positive relationships between students, parents, and school often requires an IEP team or school culture change to engage veteran parents and teachers in new and meaningful ways of interaction.
2. Parents new to the IEP process and IEP teams will have parent-school relationship needs that are very different from the needs expressed by veteran parents.
3. The degree of parent involvement in the IEP process usually produces better IEPs than those IEPs developed within limited or overzealous parent participation.
4. Through a relationship-building training protocol it is possible to develop a collaborative and meaningful relationship between parents, students, and school.

Research has demonstrated that a correlation exists between the degree of parent involvement in public schools and student achievement (Pruitt, Wandry, and Hollums, 1998). Studies have also suggested that the degree of parent participation in PTAs, parent teacher conferences, and volunteerism is largely determined by parent income, parent perceived value of education, parent's own success in the K–12 system, and by the tax base of the school district. Wealthier, suburban, and professionally educated parents are much more involved in their child's school than parents from urban and lower-income neighborhoods (Erwin and Soodal, 1995).

Parents with children who are receiving special education services present a different paradigm. The relationship between student achievements in special education is based upon the degree of participation and engagement that parents present and their sense of being an equal partner in the IEP team process.

Unlike the patterns seen between parent involvement in regular education and achievement, there are usually fewer differences between rich and poor parents, home property values, or parent education to success of children receiving special education services. While wealthier parents are able to afford legal representation or pay for advocates to attend meetings and speak on behalf of the parents and student, it has been found that a healthy relationship between the school and parents is suggested as a primary attribute to students receiving special education success.

The key to a healthy school and parent relationship seems to be solely directed toward the degree to which parents participate and are engaged and respected in the IEP process.

Unlike regular education, where student success seems to be determined by zip code, student learning in special education is related to the positive relations developed between the parents and student. Positive relations exist when the school, teachers, and district practices encourage and demonstrate a "welcoming IEP team meeting found in welcoming schools."

A welcoming school is a school that clearly presents "Parents Come In" and a school that parents want to visit. A welcoming school makes efforts to communicate openly and frequently with parents, includes parents in a variety of activities and roles such as involvement with school decisions, recommendations, and school policy and practice. Welcoming schools follow the procedures outlined in part II and are guided by mutual respect between parents and teachers. Respect is often gained by training experiences, opportunities for honest and equal participation, and real decision-making roles. Welcoming schools actively seek parent input throughout the IEP process.

Many districts and schools do not intend to present as an unwelcoming school. Many schools simply, but unfortunately, do not think about it. In some cases the fear of noncompliance to state and federal regulations and consequences of noncompliance unknowingly create an unwelcoming school culture. For example, the letter to notify parents of an upcoming IEP team meeting is not a welcoming letter; it is cold, legal, and just plain boring. Most schools do not try to be unwelcoming to parents and community stakeholders; these schools just do not realize they should be a welcoming community place.

Welcoming schools do the "little things" that help the school become an open and accommodating place. The little things are the activities that can be easily done by school staff and school practices that have a significant positive impact on parents (and school staff). Some ideas discussed in part II include "little things" like adding a little note on the official Notice of IEP Team Meeting form, a quick e-mail on student progress, a message left on a telephone answering machine telling the parents that Susie did a great job on the art project.

Little things do not take much time, and that can go a long way in building a positive and a welcoming school culture. Building relationships between school and home is a start to building a welcoming school. The relationship building starts and is maintained by the "little things": efforts made by a caring teacher, an understanding principal, and a passionate special education administrator, all of whom see the value in having parents work closely, honestly, and collaboratively with the school and through the IEP team.

The heart of relationship building is respect. Respect is the foundation of the welcoming school culture. Respect is not taught to school staffs; it is nurtured by culture and by what actually happens in school. Respect shows itself by the degree of parent and teacher interactions and relationships. Typically the more mutual respect that is developed equals the degree of the welcoming nature of the school. IEP teams likewise tend to follow suit with the school.

In nearly every case when there is a welcoming school there will also be a welcoming IEP team. This is a welcoming school culture attribute, and it shines on all or most of this school's operations and functions.

Argyris (1994) described a common conflict found in all organizations between the *espoused theory*—what an organization says it does—and the actual *theory-in-use*—the activities the organization actually does and is observed to do and not do. Often there is a chasm between what an organization says is being done (espoused theory) and what really is being done (theories-in-use).

For example, a school may say in its mission statement that all students are considered as individuals and individual student needs will be addressed (espoused theory), when in reality there are few efforts made to address individual student needs through either response to intervention (RTI) or differentiated learning (theories-in-use). Likewise in a special education description sent to parents there may be a paragraph about regular education inclusion (espoused theory), yet there is a resource room and several self-contained classrooms in the school. Inclusion occurs in P.E. and art classes (theory-in-use).

These examples show the disconnect between espoused theory and theories-in-use. Welcoming schools demonstrate little difference between what they said they do and what they actually do. Schools that have a healthy

relationship between school and parents (and students) present as what we do
is what we say we want to do; there is no disconnect.

In order to build a trustworthy and honest relationship between school
and home, there can be little difference between the espoused theory and the
theories-in-use. Every degree of conflict or disparity between the two intensi-
fies the separation of parents and school staff, and each degree of separation
creates expediential difficulties to rectify and remediate a positive change in
culture and practice.

BUILDING HOME AND SCHOOL RELATIONSHIPS

There are two paths to simultaneously travel in order to build meaningful
and purposeful relations between parents and the school. The first is to build
relations with all parents new to the IEP system. This occurs when their child
first is identified to receive special education services.

The second path is to reframe the culture and practices for parents who have
experienced the district's special education program with children already
involved with special education programming. Both paths are necessary to
address, and to address at the same time, because every district will have new
and existing parents at the same time in the special education system.

It will be impossible for a district to attempt to build a relationship, with
a welcoming culture and practices for only new parents to the system, without addressing the unique and special interests of existing parents. In many
ways the route to build collaborative parent relations is similar between the
two paths, but the paths will have significant structural differences. We will
explore both separately and then put the two directions together for a district
plan.

Relationship Building for New Parents

Parents who are just entering the special education system may have heard
stories about difficulties between home and school cooperation, piles of paperwork, ineffective IEP team meetings, lack of time for the primary teachers to individualize services, poor coordination of services across classrooms
and subject areas, and unyielding, stubborn attitudes exhibited by school
personnel.

A district or a school will rarely get a fresh or clean start, even with very
new parents. New parents to special education have a perception of what
happens at school from other parents, attending support groups, and social
networking on the Internet. New parents to the district's special education

programs often come with a lot of experience and knowledge of their child. Parents today often have a great awareness of their child's disability even shortly after the initial or first diagnosis. Many parents have a real understanding of their child's abilities and they know, from experience, what works and what does not.

Twenty years ago, teachers were taught to talk in very basic terms to parents about their child and the specific presented disability. Today, with the Internet, social networking, support groups, and publications by every disability category, parents are usually knowledgeable and aware of their child's disability.

At times, parents may have more information and awareness about the specific disability than school staff does. Parents new to the school's special education program are usually not new to the disability, albeit parents are not familiar with the policies, regulations, and methods special education in district schools provides. Hence, issues can start to develop between parents and schools right away.

When the special-needs child first gets involved with the school as a student who may need special services, this is the time to create a clear picture of district policies to the new parents. More important, this clear picture also must describe the actual, not espoused, practices toward parental engagement and participation during the child's experience in the school's special education program.

Districts are required to send information describing the special education process to all parents, explaining their rights, the expectations of all applicable rules, and district policies and practices. While important, this is not the way to start a longtime collaborative relationship. Most parents find this material overwhelming, unwelcoming, and reaffirming of the "war stories" they have heard from other special education parents.

Throughout this book, the slogan "pay now or pay later" has and will be consistently used; and, of course, it applies here. The time that district personnel commit to helping parents at this beginning time, or front loading, will go miles to start this parent-school relationship into the future. It would be easily expected that over time vast amounts of time and staff resources will be saved by having a sincere and welcoming meeting between the special education administrator or school psychologist and new parents.

This meeting should cover the basic practices of special education and WHY, not just policies or espoused theories of the district:

1. What the IEP team is and does
2. Who is on the IEP team
3. What the meetings are like

4. How ideas from the IEP team are put into practice
5. The importance of the school and home working together to reinforce generalization of skills
6. How progress is monitored and communicated
7. Basic tenets of state and federal laws applied to special education
8. What input is necessary from the parents and how the input is presented to the team
9. What kinds of services are available through the school
10. What is not provided and why
11. Explanation of the individual family service plan or the individual education plan
12. Explanation of the values and core beliefs of the district toward parent involvement and engagement and explanation of supports that can be readily available to parents to guide them through the special education process

This meeting is important, not only to begin a long-term relationship on the right foot, but to construct a positive and responsive culture (a theory-in-use) for all future team meetings. This is accomplished by the school explaining collaborative expectations of all team members.

The main point to communicate to parents is that the district honestly, sincerely appreciates and expects equal participation by the student and the parents during all educational planning and decision-making activities. It will be necessary to explicitly explain how the school wants parents and teaching staff to work closely together to improve IEP team functions and to improve the educational service delivery. These points cannot be espoused theories; they must be actual theories-in-use. They cannot be what is said—this has to be what is routinely practiced every day in the life at school.

Fish (2008) found that when parents educated themselves in special education law and the special education process, they were able to participate at higher levels than parents without this information. When parents understood the regulations and policies, they felt they were more likely to feel as an equal partner on the IEP team.

Not many parents will be able to educate themselves on hundreds of pages of special education law and district policies, albeit parents do grasp the fundamental implementation of the special education law and therefore relate well to the spirit of the law and district policies. The initial parents-administrator meeting should help clear the way for parents to gain a deeper understanding of the complex and confounding state and federal statutes and detailed district policy.

Following the initial administrator and parent meeting, it would be suggested that follow-ups occur. Many parents will attend informational-type meetings and will attend follow-ups if previous meetings were perceived by the parents to be worthwhile and their purpose was to-the-point and informative. Parents will have questions about all facets of special education, including methods of instruction, disciplinary procedures, policy and regulations, and how to handle disputes.

These questions can be easily handled during face-to-face meetings, but many questions will arise after the meeting. A welcoming school will ensure that all further questions or comments will be quickly answered by phone or e-mail. The idea is to maintain contact and reinforce a welcoming and appreciative environment leading toward building a meaningful parent-school relationship.

Regular contact between the primary teacher and the parents is critical to developing relationships and creating a welcoming school. New parents will need to positively experience a welcoming school attitude early in the process. Most new parents will have heard all kinds of stories, real and not totally real, from the "experienced parents."

The school's best defense is to remove the perception or the stereotype as soon as possible. Schools and staff must employ honest theories-in use and ensure that the school does what it says it will do. Even just a short e-mail to say "Johnny is doing well" takes little time and sends a strong cooperative-spirit message to the parents. It proves the school is welcoming; the school does what it says it will do, a theory-in-use.

Building a strong relationship at the beginning of the process will help dispel a "war story" the parents may have heard and more importantly will build a long-term school-life relationship (the life that a student has in the K–12 system) between parents, student, and the current and future schools. This type of a relationship will produce better IEPs, greatly enhance student achievement, and has the potential to make a significant difference preparing students for adult life.

Relationship Building with Existing Parents

Building a new culture, even if the school is a welcoming school, will take time and consistency. If the school has historically been an unwelcoming school; one in which there were parent complaints, disagreements at IEP team meetings, and poor attitudes, this process will be difficult. Changing perception is often more difficult than changing the culture and practices of a school or an IEP team.

Most existing parents will have experienced a disconnect between es-poused theory and theories-in-use. There will have been at least one time when a statement was made regarding a school service, or a student support that was supposed to be implemented to the student, and it did not occur. Even if there was only one time that the espoused theory was not the actual theory-in-use, there are parents who will believe that espoused theories are the norm for the team or school. Perceptions last a long time, and even if significant changes have occurred to remove the disconnect, the perception hangs on even after evidence clearly indicates otherwise.

When considering a strategy to move either from an unwelcoming or to a more welcoming school, school and team leadership and school staff must be committed to make change. The change will occur within the context of an organizational improvement initiative, one that is often seen in business orga-nizations. Such a change requires big-time work and effort, and change of this magnitude will take time. Big-time change must be continuously evaluated, consistently observable, and exhibited by all stakeholders in the educational system. See more about organizational change in appendix A.

School staff will need to be in "we need to prove our commitment" mode. A meeting to tell existing parents about the changes toward quality improve-ment and relationship building will go nowhere. Whereas this approach will have some value to parents new to special education, seasoned parents will need to see and experience change firsthand, not hear about it.

Seasoned parents talk to other special education parents; many attend con-ferences and support groups, and many parents are very informed about their child's disabilities and their rights as parents regarding the special education law. Existing parents have learned and heard almost everything that could affect special education and the nature of their child's disability.

Social networking has opened a world of communication, idea sharing, complaints, and methods to work around and with the school district, the special education law, and the services that they feel would be best and most appropriate for their child. Parents are active and they are informed.

A newsletter article about a culture change about relationship building is a big NO. It is a big NO because by doing any systemic change, the planned and potential actions are not real actions; the actions described by words will never match the perceptions held by the parents, students, and other stake-holders.

The strategy to school culture change and quality improvement is to pro-mote the initial change slowly, quietly, and without fanfare. Therefore the organization, either the IEP team, the school, or the district, needs to oper-ate the change actions; the change agents are the staff of the school and the change itself needs to be initiated within the school structure. Change should happen by actions and theories-in-use by school personnel before any action is requested from parents.

Parents are important, however, in culture change. Culture change involves a change unit or agent, whether an IEP team, a school, or an entire district. Successful quality improvement change in a change unit begins at school and with school personnel. This is done to start and demonstrate a credibility factor of serious commitment. As the change begins to transform, school administration will need to ask for parental input for real decision making and real ideas. The request for parent input must be honest and meaningful.

Information from parents must be seriously considered, and when parents are asked to be involved in decision-making activities, input and opinions must be respected. Once it may be perceived by a parent that requested input, information, and opinion is not valued, the initiative will likely fail immediately and for future efforts to involve parents in meaningful ways. It is always a good idea to involve parents for policy development, school culture development, and quality improvement initiatives at the appropriate times.

Some ideas to involve parents in a quality improvement initiative or a school culture change are limitless as long as parent involvement is requested after the school staff has initiated change as the beginning phase. There has to be evidence that change has started with the faculty and the school belief system and such change is committed to be part of the normal and daily school operations (theories-in-use). All stakeholders of the change unit including school board, administration, teaching staff, and community are on board and active as change agents. When these conditions are present, ideas for real parent involvement may include:

1. Focus groups to solicit ideas for richer school improvement and culture change
2. Parent-led advisory committees to send ideas and concerns to school administration
3. Policy review sessions to provide input on special education policy to administration and the school board
4. Training sessions for new parents to the special education program and what is expected from parents by "seasoned parents"
5. Political action committee to represent the district for local and state legislative issues
6. Regular participation in ongoing meetings and committees to share input and information from the school administration, teaching staff, community, and parents
7. Parent participation in various ad hoc meeting structures

Building relationships must involve parents in real activities. The relationships built in these activities will usually have a carry-over effect to greater parent involvement in the IEP process. Realistically not all parents are willing or want to be involved in school activities due to employment, other child responsibilities, or just do not feel they have much to offer the district. This is okay, but all parents need to really understand and believe this opportunity exists.

Building relationships with parents and with teachers as well is often an individually driven exercise. Not all parents and not all teachers come from the same mold and have the same motivation to participate and contribute during IEP team meetings and other school functions. Each change unit, the IEP team, school, or district, will have to deal with three general personality traits of special education parents, new and seasoned. The personalities of parents will have an influence on their involvement in school-related activities and with the IEP team.

PARENT PERSONALITIES

To rebuild existing relationships between school and seasoned parents, the district will need to consider the three generalized types of parents found in every school. The district must plan relationship development with all three personality types in mind. Even exceptionally good and welcoming districts will have all three parent types, so no district is immune from this mix of parent personalities.

The Bully

The Bullies are the parents who are never happy and never are satisfied by what is being provided by the school or in the IEP. Every effort to work with a Bully falls apart early in the IEP plan and with the delivery of services. Often the Bully will bring an advocate or perhaps more appropriately labeled as a mob henchman for the sole purpose of expressing enhanced and rigorous displeasure. The degree of displeasure usually relates to the lack of district services that the Bully and Bully Advocate *know* is right for the student. Bullies do not mind long IEP meetings and are often satisfied that there is little common ground between the school and the Bully in the assessment and recommendations for acquiring school services.

Lack of common ground, in the mind of the Bully, means that the Bully can say, "Boy, I really advocated for my kid." The Bully believes that IEP goals should cover every imaginable aspect of living, gain the very most minutes per week of related services, get every related service, and have every supplemental aid and support ever known.

The grand prize is getting one-to-one services, even when contrary to expert opinion. Bully IEPs rarely work for students, because there is little continuity between home and school built into the IEP. Most times one-to-one services and extraordinary minutes per week take the student out of content area instruction, and additional minutes per week of services have no therapeutic value. The student suffers.

Teachers are afraid of Bully threats and demands; administrators nicely respond to meaningless and sometimes detrimental requests made by the Bully. The student's needs are not being met, and any collaboration between the Bully and the team will be misconstrued as irrelevant by the Bully. Bullies do not communicate, they tell; and they make threats. For students, the parents' level of dissatisfaction will negate any efforts made by the teacher or school to open new possibilities and educational opportunities.

Bullies are very difficult to deal with, and change is rare. In many cases, Bullies protect themselves from change by their previous threatening behavior and demanding history. This protection is reinforced by school staff, because school staff will treat Bullies in a way that encourages the Bully to carry on the bully role. Teachers can become afraid of the Bully and then give in to the Bully, so the Bully gets what the Bully wants and the behavioral patterns are just reinforced.

The author remembers doing a parent training session on developing parent-school collaboration, the Hopes and Dreams Model (Lentz, 2004) with a mother and father, both Bullies in attendance. The Bullies would nod their heads at suggestions to work collaboratively as team members and to equally share and listen during team meetings. In fact the Bullies thanked me for the training. A month later at their child's three-year IEP team meeting that the author led, the Bullies were, well, just Bullies—one month after the training in which they expressed their appreciation!

To deal with Bullies, the reinforcing pattern of their behavior needs to be interrupted. The interruption does not have to occur in all situations, only in one or two unexpected events or activities at a time. Additionally, the school staff needs to stop encouraging the Bully behavior by responding out of fear or consternation to all the bully tactics.

A powerful interruption of the Bully behavior is for the IEP team chair to simply redirect a Bully demand, for example, "We are not there yet; we need to hear from the teacher or the psychologist first." Another Bully interruption may be, "As you know, we will discuss that later in the agenda." This type of a response clearly undermines the control the Bully wants in the meeting and questions the knowledge base of the Bully. This works because the Bully should know the agenda of the IEP team meeting and the Bully did not get his/her way at least at this time.

The goal of the IEP chair is to interrupt the balance of the Bully a little and in subtle ways. The leader can keep asking for on-topic input on how things are seen at home and in the community without asking for services or accommodations; just an observed report. The Bully will not change overnight, but the Bully can mollify the attack mode as school staff begins to not give in to Bully demands, and as the chair keeps the Bully a little off balance during the IEP meeting and other events in which the Bully operates.

The author recalls a situation when a speech therapist was recommending a reduction of minutes per week of one-on-one speech therapist to student time. The reason for the recommendation was to encourage the student with ASD to have more opportunities to verbally communicate with peers within typical school environments. The Bully parents were going wild: more minutes per week of one-on-one is the goal. Finally the speech therapist said, "I thought we were interested in having Johnny talk and interact with his classmates. He can't do that if he spends all his time with me." The therapist looked at the Bully parents and said, "What do you really want?" The parents agreed that peer communication interactions were important and the team, as a team, was able to build social interactions into the supplemental aids and support section of the IEP with the speech therapist monitoring implementation and progress from a distance.

The Bully parents did not change much right away, but once they were able to understand the logic from the speech therapist and the commitment from the team, the bullying started to fade. This one interruption seemed to start a small but significant change.

The Agreer

The Agreers are parents that have the "deer-in-the-headlights" look. Sometimes the Agreer will be seen with a forced little smile that looks like more effort than an actual smile. The Agreers are just the opposite of the Bully—they are simply passive. Agreers nod their heads when appropriate, say little, and agree with what everyone else says. Most will respond to a direct question but provide little spontaneous information related to their child or the IEP topics. Often Agreers feel the teachers and school personnel know much more than the parents do, and therefore prefer to keep quiet in fear of making a mistake.

Agreers may voice concern and some emotion to others outside of the school environs, but at school they will sit through a team meeting, agree with almost everything that is said, and usually provide little related information regarding their child. Agreers generally do not communicate IEP-related information, and they offer little to the outcome of IEP team meetings.

The Agreers like a short and to-the-point IEP team meeting. Many Agreers do have a positive and cheerful personality and are happy to share part of this personality during the meeting as long as such trait sharing does not influence or contribute to the IEP discussion. There have been times when an Agreer is funny, shares humor, and expresses concerns in the lives of others outside of the IEP team.

It is important to understand that these displays of personality are a cover for their perceived inadequacies of IEP knowledge, school services, or even their innate knowledge of their child. Another cover used by the Agreer is their attempt to be "part of the team": the Agreer will offer opinions, and even strong opinions, about topics far removed from the IEP-related topics. The Agreer wants to be a good team member, but generally does not believe that he or she can make any contributions to the team. The personality and off-task opinions mask their anxiety and fear of not doing or saying what the team wants the Agreers to say or do.

The Agreers' children also suffer because there is no sharing of information, no desires or outcomes expressed for the present or future, and little sharing of what is important for the child or the family. While the school staff may like the Agreer because there is little fear of conflict or disagreement, school staff need to be cognizant of the balance and worth that parents bring to the team. Schools do not always get it right, but together with parents, the team can construct functional IEPs.

Like the Bully, it is difficult to change the Agreer. Someone cannot simply say, "Okay, from now on you know what you are talking about and you have no fear of being wrong." It will take tact and gentle pushing from the IEP team leader to bring about a behavior pattern of confidence. The leader of the team will have to understand the protective cover used by the Agreers and attempt to channel the cover into productive discussion and contributions to the team.

This behavior change can start with the team chair helping the Agreer to share some thoughts about their child and one or two general outcomes they hope to see in the future based upon their recent observation of their child in natural settings. The chair can make a distinction between the observations at school, a contrived environment, and the comparison to real events and environs, which could be very important. The members of the team will also be interested in the Agreer's thoughts, since the information will be new and different from the school data and findings.

Meaningful responses can also be requested after the Agreer has offered a remote opinion. The team leader can then ask the Agreer for an opinion on a topic recently discussed on the team agenda. For example, the team chair can say, "Thanks, that was a well-thought-out observation, but how do you feel about Sally seeing the school psychologist once a week to talk about appropriate social interactions with her peers? Do you think this will help Sally maintain friends at home and school?"

A question that should always be asked by the team meeting leader is, "What are you seeing at home?" in reference to various topics being discussed. For example, "What are you seeing at home in regard to Sally playing with friends and other family members during unstructured time? We never get to see this response at school."

The team leader will need to be judicious about the timing for a forced, on-topic opinion, and it needs to be timed to not create feelings of increased inadequacy. If timed correctly and asked infrequently, Agreers' responses to questions can be unguarded and meaningful.

The author has found that Agreers benefit from the Hopes and Dreams Model (Lentz, 2004) helping them understand what to say and how to prepare for an IEP team meeting so the parents can equally participate in the team meeting as a resource, not as just an Agreer.

If the request for an opinion is too predictable, the Agreer is very good about deflecting personal thoughts and opinions. Therefore the team leader cannot request a response too often or too close to a previously asked, requested response. The leader will need to interrupt the parent behavioral patterns presented by the Agreer. This needs to be done a little at a time, and especially with the Agreer, done carefully. A skilled team leader should be able to disrupt the behavior pattern by using a request for response and on-topic opinions to effect change and not reinforce the Agreer's passive behavioral patterns.

The Collaborator

Collaborators are the A team; they are the Appreciators, Advocates, and have learned to be Aware. They understand the basic tenets of the special education laws, they have ideas of what they would like to see for their child, and they participate collaboratively during IEP team meetings, as well as with school staff outside of the team meetings. They have high expectations and demand performance, but they realize that home, school, and the community must work together to ensure student success.

Collaborators will make some teachers uncomfortable because Collaborators come into IEP team meetings prepared with proposed educational and life outcomes, and with a wide knowledge base of their child's disability. Collaborators will work cooperatively with schools to find reasonable solutions and joint outcomes. Children of Collaborators generally succeed at home, school, and in the community to a greater degree than children of other parent personality characteristics.

The Collaborator parent was probably the model the founders of IDEA pictured when they wrote into the law a mandate that parents are equal partners on the IEP team. As students are more frequently fully participating in the IEP process, many students themselves fit into characteristics common to Collaborators.

Collaborators have learned how to advocate for their child by being informed and aware of regulations, district policies, and the specific disability category. Students are more involved with the IEP team because advocacy and self-determination efforts were taught in school and at home and were employed often by Collaborator parents and transformational leaders with the entire IEP team.

Collaborator parents and students know what is expected of them during and outside of team meetings, and they are prepared to participate. Many Collaborator parents are supportive for their child to be an active participant on the team, and in some cases have helped the child lead the student's own IEP team meeting.

One mother, a Collaborator, following the steps outlined in chapter 9 in part II, prepared a written report of the newly learned skills, emerging skills, outcomes for the immediate future, and recommendations for how efforts at home could couple with the goals worked on at school. This mother presented this information like an oral summary assessment. One teacher commented to the mother after the IEP team meeting, "You have nearly written the entire IEP!"

This is the world of the Collaborator. The Collaborator goes to training; the Collaborator sees a commonality of IEP goals that mesh at home as well as at school and can be used in the community. The Collaborator knows that for this to happen it is also important for the student to express outcomes and dreams now and into the future as the student heads toward adulthood.

The Collaborator knows that the school is not always right and that it takes the school, student, and home to work together to bring out the best possible outcomes for the student. The Collaborator, parent and student, advocates for this outcome. It is possible that some school personnel may be threatened by the knowledge base and the workability of the Collaborator, but this is what is necessary for student achievement.

BUILDING RELATIONSHIPS: A DISTRICT PLAN

All three character types exist in all schools in parents new to the special education system as well as existing parents. Not every parent is going to turn into a Collaborator, but many can make steps toward being on the way. The basic relationship-building tool is training for parents as well as students and school staff, described in chapter 12.

Parent training in smaller groups along with some school staff helps the Bullies and Agreers to gain an appreciation of the law, the special education service delivery system, and the work performed by the school staff. Training will not work for all Bullies or Agreers as was seen in a previous example, but over time progress toward Collaboration can be experienced.

Such training needs to start with a session sincerely expressing the role and the importance of the working relationship between parents and school. Research readily demonstrates that collaboration and IEPs developed by a functioning IEP team result in a better educational plan than plans developed without collaboration between school and family.

It is best to hold this session with some school officials and staff and seasoned parents to send a clear and unified message to parents that the district is sincere in its efforts to develop meaningful and long-term relationships. Topics to be covered would include:

1. Role of parents and students in the IEP process, why equal participation is important, and how parents should learn ways to be prepared to present information necessary to the school and team
2. Role of the school personnel in the IEP process, assessments and evaluations used, and how school personnel analyze data and make recommendations and conclusions
3. Dialogue between school personnel, parents, and students regarding evaluative data and recommendations to support teacher and parent outcomes
4. How parents present information to the IEP team, how to utilize the "parents assessment" described in chapter 12, and how to express realistic and meaningful outcomes for team consideration
5. How students can be involved in their educational program and how to present information to the IEP team; what supports are necessary and what training is going to help the student present independently
6. How parents and school personnel monitor and determine success and skill acquisition in naturally occurring environments and events
7. How parents, students, and school personnel deal with and resolve conflicting ideas and how meaningful recommendations are developed to support student achievement
8. What happens after the IEP team meeting, what paperwork will be developed, what the time frames are for program implementation

9. What the methods are to review progress from home, school, and the community and how progress across all environments will be assessed and communicated

TRANSFORMATION: THE DISTRICT'S PLAN

As discussed earlier, the improvement for the team, school, or district is accomplished through the foresight and the vision of and by a transformational leader. The transformational leader of the IEP team or school should ask the following question: "Isn't it better to teach parents, students, and school staff what to report and how to fully participate in the IEP team meeting and to chair collaborative IEP team meetings, than it is to undergo grievances, hearings, and due process?" The answer should be clear; it is cheaper, with less stress on resources, financial as well as staff time, to work in front of the IEP system than it is to deal with a few grievances and costly due process at the back end; pay now or pay later.

At conferences and in professional journals, teachers and administrators learn and read about the best ways to handle disputes. Almost all reflect on legal procedures, formal hearings, and sometimes informal mediation. The author and transformational IEP team leaders agree that it is necessary to disrupt the increasing cycle of disputes.

Yet pundits and special education and legal experts continue to exploit the cycle of disputes by dealing with the back end of the problem—hearings, mediation, and due process. Every problem espoused by these professionals and attorneys occurs after the fact of a dispute. Few, if any, ever talk about the front end of the IEP team meeting. The front end includes developing transformational team leaders; training for school staff, parents, and students; and developing collaborative cultures.

This is why it is important to build family and school relations as an ongoing partnership working on behalf of one student and one child. Fixing the problem or the dispute through the typically sung songs of facilitation, mediation, due process, and even further along the legal opera fixes the dispute and the relationship *only once.*

This would be fine if the child had only one IEP team meeting in the student's K–12 career. Unfortunately for the advocates of back-end efforts to solve issues through facilitation, mediation, and due process, there are many successive IEP team meetings. The anger, frustration, and lack of a collaborative relationship remain even when the previous dispute is "fixed." One-time fixes are a waste of time. Sure, one problem at one time may be decided for or against the parents or the school, but this decision will do nothing to make the next time any better—probably with less cooperation.

Developing positive and effective parent-teacher, home-school relationships can and will last the school life of the child with disabilities. The author has repeatedly seen parents looking forward to their child's IEP team meeting, actively discussing student gains and experiences, and seeing results of school assessments and perceptions by school staff. Likewise, the author has experienced the joy and satisfaction of teachers understanding the life of the student outside of school.

ANALYSIS

1. How do espoused theory and theories-in-use apply to school and parent relationships?
2. Why do parents retell and relate to "war stories" that may not even have affected them or their children?
3. What are you going to do to start a process of relationship building in your school with your parents and school staff?

EVALUATION

1. What can you do to reduce the disconnect between espoused theory and theories-in-use in your school?
2. What will you do to further engage new parents in school activities and hopefully develop richer IEP team participation?
3. Who and in what areas will you need to work hardest to promote a transformational change in your school system?
4. What can you do to increase staff enthusiasm for transformational change?
5. Where do you see potential for new transformative leaders in your school?
6. What will you need to add to the ideas to incorporate into parent meetings?

4

How Teams Miss Opportunities

KEY POINTS

1. Good IEP teams and good IEPs stop greatness from occurring.
2. IEP teams often miss opportunities to construct great IEPs because teams do not feel they can change the manner in which the IEP team can operate.
3. Opportunities for improvement occur by applying principles of learning organization and transformational leadership.
4. Organizational change is necessary to reduce missed opportunities for greatness.
5. Issues surrounding lack of time, too many IEPs, and fear of consequences in the IEP system are manageable when the Theory of Missed Opportunities is understood and applied.

IEP teams miss opportunities to effectively develop great IEPs for five primary reasons: allocation of time, unawareness of the ways to develop great IEPs, too many IEPs to write and chair, paperwork requirements within mandatory time frames, and fear of regulatory consequences. All of these issues are understandable, yet all cripple efforts for IEP teams to function at their best.

Most IEP teams miss opportunities, but the results are usually not devastating—good IEPs are still constructed. However, the point is that good usually means that great IEPs are not in the realm of possibility; good is okay, therefore good becomes the enemy of greatness. When good is accepted, great IEPs cannot happen because opportunities for greatness are missed. Unfortunately good IEPs usually mean the IEP meets the basic requirements as

45

I hate this book!

expressed in state and federal special education law. The laws do three things to restrict great IEPs from occurring: first, laws are based upon the most minimum of standards and quality is not a part of minimum standards; second, the laws do not define the degree to which leadership applies; and lastly, there is no consideration for the transformational leader that is responsible for the operation of the IEP team. For too many IEP teams, good is good enough, and good means the minimum letter of the law has been accepted and met.

While *the letter* of the law is important, it is *the spirit* of the special education law that moves a good IEP team and a good IEP to greatness. The spirit of the law is expressed by exceeding good, allowing quality to shape the potential of student achievement in meaningful and functional ways.

The spirit of the laws means that equal participation by parents and students really occurs and that parents and students are respected, are given a real voice, and the school supports parents and students in all possible ways, including training, active engagement, and opportunities to serve and contribute.

It is the spirit of the law that evokes quality and a deeper and richer IEP team experience for all team members. Greatness is inhibited by the acceptance of the letter of the law. As seen in chapter 1, the fallacy of the IEP team chair characterized as the Lion was the overindulgence of the letter of the law. The Lion operated by such an extent to the letter of the law that the letter of the law restricted the operation of the IEP team from actually doing what the law required. For example, in the discussion of extended school year (ESY), the Lion's overly rigorous criteria for providing ESY overrode the team's recommendation for ESY due to demonstrated regression the previous year. But meeting the letter of the law only to save the school district from all the bad stuff that can happen devastates discussion, problem solving, creating new ideas, and seeking new strategies that all destroy student success and achievement.

To understand the ramifications of factors that inhibit IEP greatness—time, too many IEPs, paperwork requirements, lack of awareness of great IEPs, and fear of consequences—educators need to understand the Theory of Missed Opportunities.

THEORY OF MISSED OPPORTUNITIES

The Theory of Missed Opportunities consists of two co-joined or abutting circles that represent in the left circle the IEP team, school, or district organization, and in the right circle the individual school employee, administrator, and specialists. Much like a Venn diagram (see figure 4.1), the co-joined area

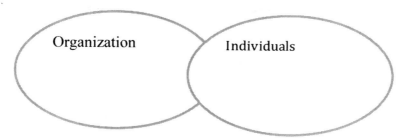

Figure 4.1.   Theory of missed opportunities: Two components.

symbolizes the degree of making opportunities work during the IEP process; the smaller the overlapped area, the increased likelihood of missed opportunities. The larger the area of overlap, the greater the likelihood of opportunities for great IEPs. This theory is based on the characteristics and the interaction of the organization as a whole and as individuals within the organization. It is important to understand the basic framework of the organization and the individual to further conceptualize how this theory creates missed opportunities and enhances the ability to create great IEP teams and IEPs.

The Organization

The Theory of Missed Opportunities articulates the organization as the prevailing school culture and the daily norms of the school (see figure 4.2). School culture and norms make up the nature of the organization. Culture is characterized by how the organization examines and treats mistakes; expresses fear or acceptance of the unknown or new ideas, change, and innovation; and encourages or discourages teams, schools, or district to take risks.

The daily norms of the organization are assessed by the gap or the overlap seen between espoused theory and theories-in-use. The degree to which each of these characteristics is evident in an organization and the degree of overlap of theories-in-use, the more likely the organization will be inclined to move toward either a culture of opportunities or a culture of missed opportunities.

Figure 4.2.   The organization.

One can argue that staying the same does not harm the organization, but staying the same creates missed opportunities for school and IEP enhancement and improvement that may lead to enhanced opportunities for student achievement.

The Individual

The circle on the right in figure 4.3 represents the individual in the organization. The individual is the teacher, administrator, or school specialist. The individual is characterized by attitudes and perceptions of the individual employee. Attitudes are different from culture. Attitudes are individually determined, preserved, and changed by the perception of the person, but not usually by an organizational effort to do so. The organization's (team, school, or district) culture can have some effect upon attitudes, but attitudes are created by the stakeholder or the members in the organization.

Attitudes are characterized by the degree to which the person in the organization ascertains to personal beliefs that new concepts will or will not work, that change is threatening or exciting to the individual, that new ideas create more work without personal benefit or present as a positive paradigm shift, and ideas and new concepts are just another mandate or an opportunity to pursue greatness. Generally these attitudes and perceptions are formed and framed by the individual employee, not solely by the organization.

This is evident because there is such a wide array of different individual responses and reactions to the same change in organizational structure that the organization itself cannot be the primary catalyst for such responses. This is easily seen by a district's implementation of response to intervention (RTI); the district presents knowledge and expectations in the same way, yet there are individual attitudes in every imaginable degree, negative to positive. Nothing different is presented with the culture, and everything different in attitude.

Figure 4.3.   The individual.

Culture and Attitude Interactions

When one normally considers opportunities missed by the IEP team and attempts are made to reduce such missed opportunities, what immediately comes to mind are typical responses: This will not work, we have tried this already, how many times do we do the same thing in different ways, I have been doing this for ten years—are you now saying this isn't good enough?

The difficulty with culture and attitudes is manifested by the perception that there is a lack of time to make significant change, beliefs that the district has policies that can't be changed, evidence that parents get everything they want no matter what the school sees and says, the IEP agenda is set and can't be changed, or my co-teachers will never go for anything different than has been done for the past fifteen years. These are the typical reasons for not engaging in organizational development.

So the Theory of Missed Opportunities posits that in order to reduce missed opportunities for great IEP teams and great IEPs to happen, one cannot just change the typical reasons to continue with marginal or mediocre IEP teams and IEPs. One cannot just change the manifestations such as too little time; unknown methods to improve IEP teams; too many IEPs to lead, write, or attend; paperwork mandates; and the fear of regulatory consequences. Change must come from the interaction and the overlap of culture and attitudes found defined by the Venn diagram.

The area of overlap needs to be enlarged, demonstrating greater integration between the organization and the individual, or between culture and attitudes. The theory posits that changing the amount of time to complete writing IEPs or implementing new district policies, for example, will not be effective when dealing with a specific issue in isolation from working with both the organization's culture and the individual's attitudes.

Change to greatness or organizational improvement can only occur when the organization (the school) and the attitudes (individual employees of the school) work in concert to advocate and promote systemic change toward not missing opportunities for greatness. To do this, two big things need to simultaneously happen: the *organization* must move toward being a learning organization and the *individual* toward being a transformational leader. See figure 4.4.

A common misconception is that only a few organizations are real learning organizations and only people in upper management can become transformational leaders. Both impressions are very wrong: all organizations, large-small, business-educational, private-public have the capacity to be a learning organization. Likewise all persons within an organization have the ability to

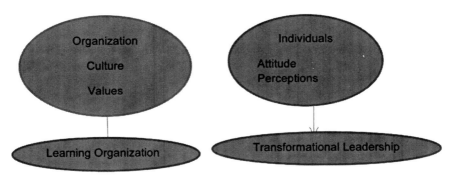

Figure 4.4. Movement of the organization and the individual.

be transformational leaders. Leadership is not management—this is a very important distinction to understand.

Individuals to Transformational Leaders

When people lead, they move persons toward a visionary end. Leadership occurs in good and not-as-good ways. Leadership can occur in a small meeting, or on a special project, in an IEP team meeting, and during any everyday activities. Leadership is seen throughout the organizational structure; when one says "I have an idea, let's try . . .," or "I think we need to do this to help . . .," leadership occurs as the change agent motivates others to risk change and find new ways to do something different and hopefully better. Management is when a superior tells a subordinate what to do (although good managers can be good leaders).

The concepts that most anyone can be a leader and that anyone can be a transformational leader are important ideas to understand. It is also difficult to think of many employees (individuals) that can be leaders at the same time, yet this is what transformational leadership attempts to do.

Each employee will have transformational specializations that together with other individuals specializing in other areas bring a complete package. This may be seen during ad hoc committees working on a specific project. One individual will bring a specialization in educational strategy, another in motivating others, while another has skills to bring external stakeholders into the scope of the project. All have characteristics of transformational leadership, but together the various specialties round out a total package for quality improvement and rarely a missed opportunity.

One example of the breadth of transformative leaders working together was seen during a series of planning meetings to develop a mentoring program to improve and retain new special education teachers in a school district. One administrator was a proponent of a peer mentoring system, and she had completed a rich review of peer mentoring approaches used in education and in business and could apply attributes to working with other staff. Another was a special education teacher who was keenly aware of the demands and confusion experienced by new special education teachers and could apply attributes to working with other staff.

The director of special education was knowledgeable of the special education regulations and of a state initiative to support more training for all new teachers and could apply attributes to working with other staff. A regular education teacher was aware of the complexity of the laws and the difficulty of meaningful inclusion for many special education students and could apply attributes to working with other staff.

This group met on a regular basis for about three months. Each member had an attitude of the importance of the project and a perception of the method through which new teachers could be supported and guided during their first three years on the job in this district.

Each member worked closely with other team members, and each member attempted to learn more about the situation from research and best practices across the country. While the team members worked and met as a committee, they also worked (led) independently to solicit buy-in from other teachers and staff, accumulated more information from others, and integrated best practices into proposed school-specific norms. The goal was the same for all members, but the methods, practices, and knowledge utilized were very different.

Through the individual attitudes of transformation and the necessity to modify the culture in the organization (the school district), the transformational leaders communicated to the school staff, came together as a group with a shared vision for implementation, promoted the end result, sought school board and district administration approval, and implemented a comprehensive new teacher mentoring program that focused on retention, adjustment of new teachers to the school district, and safety zones for new teachers to ask questions, voice concerns, and get help without fear of evaluation and judgment made by others.

Many transformational leaders, at the same time, took this project to a place far surpassing the original expectations of this ad hoc school committee.

Changing the culture also means changing individual attitudes. If individual perceptions do not reflect the values and beliefs of the learning organization, change will be shortsighted and will fail. Attitudes and individual perceptions must transform in alignment with the organizational changes seen by the development of the learning organization.

It is nearly impossible for the organization to adjust its philosophy and practices and to develop attributes of a learning organization without an adjustment of personnel beliefs and individual change in attitudes and perceptions. Individual perceptions and attitudes change by organizational (change unit) movement toward the learning organization. Efforts to promote transformed individual attitudes and perceptions often lead to a better individual understanding of the need for quality improvement and great IEP teams and student IEPs.

Changing the Organizational Culture: The Learning Organization

Changing the organizational culture is an exercise and a study far beyond the intent and scope of this writing, but the author has provided several references for interested readers to pursue this important topic more fully. The basic idea of culture change is that the IEP team, school, or district work toward becoming a learning organization. See figure 4.4. A learning organization is in simple terms a system that is totally aware of its integration within its own environment, where the environment is safe for risk taking and sharing of ideas to promote organizational performance, and to foster organizational creativity and creative tension to provide organizational energy. See appendix A for a more detailed description of learning organization and other organizational theories.

It is the belief and goal of embracing a learning organization initiation made by a district or a school, or even an IEP team, that will most likely produce meaningful culture change. Culture change creates tension between previous and forthcoming practices. Tension embraces the potential of new ways, promoting increased effectiveness and culture change.

However, tension, like a bungee cord, can stretch, but always wants to return to its original state. Tension is important to balance the stability of the old ways that have been proven techniques; to stretch beyond its natural state but not so far that it completely loses its original shape. Tension permits change, while it supports conceptual beliefs and values of the origination and yet offers the promise of increased improvement and greatness.

The culture change, even in very small increments, generates enough organization tension to create a norm realignment to reject the idea of good IEPs and start a process to expect great IEP team meetings and therefore great IEPs. Admittedly this can be a long process and will have significant ups and downs, but on the other hand so will the alternative of doing nothing.

Usually persons think making no change means no extra effort, but if one were to realistically look at making no change and maintaining the status quo, one would find huge amounts of effort to maintain the current status for no enhanced benefit.

With a little more than the normal effort to maintain the current operation of an IEP team, school, or district, the organization could make strides toward being a learning organization. A functional learning organization is one that makes a concerted effort to share a vision for the future, shares common values, celebrates accomplishments, recognizes that mistakes are essential in the learning toward organizational improvement. Senge (1990) defined a learning organization by five disciplines: shared vision, personal mastery, mental models, team learning, and systems thinking.

Senge's five disciplines begin with a shared vision, which is a forward and projected look into the possibilities of an organization that is commonly held and embraced by stakeholders of an organization. Obviously a shared vision is not a statement made by management, but a projection of opportunities and possibilities that may exist and are powerful enough to be held as commonly shared visions or organizational attributes.

Examples of shared visions in the case of the IEP team efforts to become a learning organization to produce great IEP teams may include a common belief that parents are experts in the lives of their children and what parents communicate during IEP team meetings will be valued to the highest esteem. A shared vision may be that a school will value total inclusion of special education students into all areas of the school experience. A district may share a vision for immersion of differentiated learning in all educational environments within the district.

These values are not merely official statements. These shared visions are constructed over time and within the framework of the beliefs and values of the persons in the organization and by the organization itself. This is a meshing of the organization and individual to increase the common area seen in figure 4.1.

The second attribute of a learning organization is personal mastery. Personal mastery is pictured as the tension between what is happening in an organization today and the shared vision of tomorrow. There should be tension, meaning necessary efforts to keep the organization from running away with the shared vision while leaving the current status of an organization and individuals behind yet moving cautiously ahead of the current status.

Personal mastery occurs when persons in the organization value the shared vision. Then stakeholders must understand that need to experience changes in their work life to achieve the shared vision. Personal mastery creates the tension necessary to hold today and tomorrow in check and within realms of possibility.

Personal mastery is learning both on the organizational and individual side. Personal mastery can be seen at the IEP team level when the team is charged with implementing a new strategy for students with autism, or in a school where RTI is a shared vision, but many teachers do not understand its ramifications and how it can be infused into the existing school structure.

Likewise a district has shared a vision for the retention of special educators for three and more years of employment; personal mastery indicates that change is necessary and change will occur and create tension between the district's operations of today and its vision for the future.

The third of Senge's disciplines are mental models. Mental models are usually employee mindsets that get in the way of the learning organization and changing culture. Mental models are ways for employees and stakeholders to try to understand the organization's interactions with the industry's environment, the business climate, the technology in the field, and the persons in the working structure.

These mental models are a flawed system to explain to the employee why things happen in today's environment. Mental models are the thoughts of how employees think about new ways in the organization.

Senge posits that mental models are never complete and always changing; they are usually not accurate, are usually oversimplified, and are usually incorrect. Mental models need to be checked in a learning organization—checked often by shared vision and personal mastery.

Mental models are easily seen throughout an organization, but rarely are they addressed. Following a previous example of RTI being introduced into an IEP team, school, or district, mental models are obvious: "This is too complicated and will never work"; "This is just another way to put all those special education kids in my classroom." These thoughts are transparent to others, and they hold back progress that may propel hope and opportunity for many students.

Mental models can be seen on IEP teams when a recommendation is dismissed under the guise that the evaluations are never any good, the student cannot learn, or the parents don't see what the student is doing in the classroom. At the school level a mental model may be that inclusion will not work for severely disabled students, that these students need to be in a self-contained classroom during the school day. Mental models are evident in districts as they implement a new math curriculum or if there are changes to state or federal mandates.

Fourth as a learning organization discipline is team learning. Team learning is basically that: learning as a subpart of the organization to further enhance the shared vision and personal mastery and to check obsolete or negative mental models. Team learning is really a part of the shared vision. Personal mastery tells us that change is necessary to work toward a shared vision, and shared vision relates to the potential of the organization, but team learning helps to abate the harmful effects of negative mental models.

Team learning in IEP teams may occur when members of IEP teams internally discuss, research, and share ideas to help parents and teachers feel more comfortable during the team meetings, or at school to discuss, share, and problem-solve methods to help regular education teachers understand effective strategies for students with disabilities in their classrooms.

At the district level team learning may be seen through efforts to develop relationships with local businesses to offer vocational training opportunities outside of school for students with disabilities. Team learning is not classroom learning; it is sharing of ideas, discussing possibilities, and developing rapport toward the shared vision while dispelling interfering mental models.

The last discipline is what Senge called systems thinking. Systems thinking is the condition that an organization is affected by any and all actions taken or not taken. One change will impact all others. Senge also used a model of an open system to describe systems thinking.

The open system is never completed in its quest toward the shared vision. This open system promotes norms and values that appreciate innovation and ideas that may better serve the organization. Systems thinking helps IEP teams look for new and encouraging methods to plan the instruction of students and it helps schools realize that a change in curriculum will affect IEP; a change in district organization will ripple throughout the school organization. Transformational leaders need to understand systems thinking and consider all possibilities when looking to promote even a simple culture change.

The learning organization does change culture, and culture is changed by transformational leaders. Even good organizations need a continuous culture change, because under systems thinking, the system is never done growing. In this discussion of going from a team or school doing good IEPs to doing great IEPs, the culture and the organization will help the individual change attitudes and perceptions, just like individual attitudes can impact organizational culture. In figure 4.5 the discussion now goes from the organization

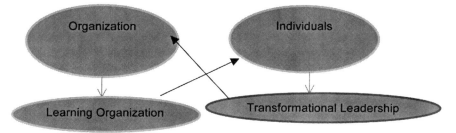

Figure 4.5.   Outcomes of organization and individual movement.

and the learning organization to the individual—the student, parent, teacher, principal, specialty service personnel, and all stakeholders.

MISSED OPPORTUNITIES TO FINDING GREAT POSSIBILITIES

The two principals of the Theory of Missed Opportunities—organization and individuals—come together to enhance possibilities of great IEP teams and IEPs. The Theory of Missed Opportunities is based on the development of a learning organization and development of individual attitudes through transformational leadership. These components must work together; one would be impossible to maintain without the other.

The change agent is the transformational leader who must not only guide the individuals and the organization through the difficult beginnings of these processes, but be able to start such processes with enthusiasm and a sense of accomplishing outcomes and the elements of the shared vision.

Transformational leadership is necessary to actualize the learning organization as a piece of the continuous quality enhancement program. Senge (1990) posits the open system as a process of never-ending organizational improvement. This open system defines organizations' intent to self-improve, promote the learning organization concept, and to permit the individuals within the organization to ascertain employee alignments of attitudes and perception.

The open system allows individuals to pursue their own interests as long as these interests are connected to the organization's shared vision; mistakes are tolerated with the understanding that new ideas and transformation is in itself a learning process, and mistakes lead to greater and deeper understanding of the organizational initiatives. In the same vein as organizational learning, the open system clearly espouses a never-ending process; improvement is continual and eternal.

MISSED OPPORTUNITIES

In this Theory of Missed Opportunities, opportunities for greatness are missed usually because the culture has not changed to meet the current needs of the purpose of the organization, and because transformational leadership is either absent or unknown. When the organization embraces the learning organization and individuals to strive toward transformation, the organization and the individuals in the organization can now address the issues that interfere with most manifestations of "why things don't get better." See figure 4.5. Five manifestations will be discussed: allocation of time, unawareness of ways to improve, too many IEPs, paperwork requirements, and fear of regulatory consequences.

Time

Time is an issue because there is simply not enough time for teaching staff to do all that they need to do. One of the most common complaints about teaching is that there is not enough time for teachers to have shared planning time with other teachers, to meet with in-school specialists, and to maintain contact with parents. Time can greatly interfere with quality and can be a missed opportunity for greatness.

IEP transformational team leaders need to understand time as a period or duration, not as a single moment or like a clock. Time is an expanse, not a single moment or event. For example, it is important to think of time as it impacts teachers over days and perhaps even a school year, rather than think of time only as hours and minutes.

The IEP leader must think of time as a continuum starting from the point of an IEP being implemented and ending with student goal attainment, not as "I need to get through this IEP team meeting in less than two hours." Time is a complex yet interfering concept. Usually it is "the concept of time" that disrupts the quality cycle, not actually time itself. We all tend to think about time as a clock, our perception of losing time, not thinking of time as a sequence of a duration and long-term event.

If time were considered for trying to get everything in place for an IEP meeting, or to write the IEP, or to get all the evaluations completed for an IEP meeting, time is short and time will be a missed opportunity. If, however, the team leader were to consider time to train the parents, students, and staff to engage in a collaborative team meeting, one in which parents and students are prepared to participate in the process, then time is saved because the duration of the time will work well into the future. Time is duration.

Opportunities are missed for great IEPs due to a variety of reasons, but generally because educators miss the intent of the special education law. In other words, educators miss opportunities because educators do not conceptualize the concept of time to produce great IEPs. Most educators cannot see the great IEP, but they perceive the time taken to construct a great IEP. Time is going to be consumed, but when and where time is consumed is controlled by the educator, not the situation.

The idea for many people and often teachers is that it is better to pay for time later, because "right now, I don't have time." It is a hard concept to understand that it may be easier and better to pay early and have time later to do something else.

This concept works this way. If an IEP team leader were to spend time to train parents and students to become engaging participants using a collaborative IEP model, and to train school staff to understand the collaborative IEP, the time expended for this training would probably save time later if there were issues with the implementation of the IEP. This is the pay-now part. The pay later occurs when conflict or disagreement occurs after the IEP team meeting, and usually the team either must meet again or redirect the IEP.

The choice of pay now or pay later is up to the IEP team leader. It has nothing to do with the special education law or district policy. It is the leader's discretion of when to use time for the leader and the leader's team. The author has found it generally true that paying early makes the most time sense, rather than waiting to pay time later. This is true because when one pays early or now, the leader knows exactly what and how much will need to be paid. This time can be scheduled and it can be allocated in usable and available blocks of time.

The pay-later paradigm is always a guessing game because the leader will never know what is to be paid until the time to pay comes. If the time comes to pay and payment is time in the form of a grievance or a hearing, then time is paid at an extremely high rate. If a payment results in another IEP team meeting, time is paid by all team members, and should time be required to rewrite parts of the IEP, then again time is expended without opportunity to plan or ration time to be spent until pay later.

Not at all times does pay now completely eliminate a pay-later case. But it has been generally felt that when efforts to prevent issues popping up later are made, then time spent is minimized, is planned, and is allocated within times available for the leader. When the IEP team leader can plan time under pay now, time utilization has just become greatly improved—for the leader, parents, and the team.

Pay-later cases almost always are missed opportunities for great IEPs. This happens because the time to adequately prepare the team to produce great IEPs does not occur. As seen in the following chapters in part II, training, welcoming, and attitudes toward the IEP team meeting are absent, and this inhibits the team from optimal performance.

It is very similar to a football coach not taking time before the scheduled games to have the players get into shape and practice plays. The IEP team leader must get the team in shape and practice to construct IEPs that really are great by meeting individual needs of students. Time is better spent up front, in the beginning rather than later and after the fact. Most professionals would rather plan their time (pay now) than have unexpected time constraints thrown at them requiring everything else to be dropped to deal with some issue that could have been prevented.

what?
planet.

Unawareness of Ways to Improve the IEP Team and IEPs

Many educators do not think they are able to make transformational or structural changes with IEP teams and the IEP. Many administrators and teachers
have only seen one or two ways to conduct an IEP team meeting, and IEPs are
set in stone at the district level. Change is often not considered. Furthermore,
the interpretation of the special education laws leaves, in the mind of many
school staff, an inability to improve what appears to be a prescribed method
of running the IEP team and constructing IEPs that are assumed to be set in
stone.

By understanding the Theory of Missed Opportunities, and recognizing
how the organization and the individual can impact positive change, school
officials can now see that change is a possibility and one that will embrace
greatness in meeting the interests and needs of students with disabilities. The
Theory of Missed Opportunities brings the two most important change elements into the working picture of educators: the learning organization and
transformational leadership.

As an IEP team, or a school, or even a district, employing the principles
of these elements, change is possible. Albert Humphrey (Ansoff, 1987) suggested that systemic change follow a SWOT analysis.

The SWOT analysis is a technique used to analyze where an organization
stands in preparation for change or to assess its position for growth. The
SWOT is completed by a team of stakeholders familiar with the change unit.
Community members, teachers, parents, and school board and administrative members begin by analyzing the internal operations of an IEP team. The
internal operations are the strengths (S) and weaknesses (W). For quality
improvement initiatives, a sample IEP would identify all the strengths the
sample IEP team demonstrates and determine its weaknesses.

An example of a sample IEP strengths and weaknesses assessment might
look like:

Strengths	Weaknesses
Goals matched recommendations on assessments and evaluations	Time lines for goal completion were too extended
Evaluations completed on time	Administrator not present at IEP
Transition planning was discussed and reasonable recommendations made	Supplemental aids and supports were not very comprehensive in relation to needs of student

These reviews are considered by only looking at the internal operations
seen in the school's IEP teams and on the IEPs. The team members would

then analyze the strengths and weaknesses in terms of celebrating what the team does well and would plan to abate the weaknesses.

The next step is to analyze the external and environmental factors of the same sample IEP team; these would evolve from a sample team member discussion on the opportunities (O) presented to the team as well as the threats (T). This discussion tends to be more subjective and opinionated, but both are necessary to complete this four-step process of team functionability.

An example of a sample IEP strengths and weaknesses assessment might look like:

Opportunities   Threats
Increased community awareness   Integration to some content classes
  for vocational placement in   is limited by teacher attitudes
  community seems possible in
  nearby grocery store

By completing the SWOT analysis, the same team can have an objective-subjective review of the current operation of the sample team and assess the degree to which the team accepts and understands change.

Change can happen at any level in an organization. An exercise like the SWOT can propel an IEP team, school, or district into a change unit and engage it in a continuous quality improvement initiative to work on something even as small as the IEP team or as large as a district-wide project.

Too Many IEPs to Lead and Write

In many schools this would be the number one problem faced by special education staff and administrators. It is true that IEPs take considerable time to write, but the time necessary for constructing great IEPs is dependent upon the information gained at the IEP team meeting. When information is presented according to desired and collaborative outcomes, IEP development becomes easier and more efficient than when information is off track and unguided. This process is significantly enhanced by understanding concepts of the learning organization and transformational leadership.

These essential elements are the basis for part II that will help transformational leaders to chair the IEP within a context of transformation and the learning organization. A school or a district may not be able to cut back on the number of IEPs that need to be scheduled, chaired, or written, but the school or district can sure change the method employed to accomplish the leading and the writing of the IEP.

Following the steps described in part II, IEP meetings should last for about one to one and a half hours, not two or three or sometimes over a course of days. Furthermore, much of the writing of the IEP can be developed at the meeting from the work that is done in preparation for the meeting.

The point is not time and the quantity of IEPs may be too demanding, the point is to change the methods of accomplishing the task with the mindset of learning organizational and leadership while engaging in a quality improvement effort to present great IEPs. Yes, it can be done, and it needs to be done; student success demands it.

Paperwork Requirements

It seems that the more the federal rule changes attempt to reduce paperwork requirements in special education, the amount of paper seems to increase, but most notably, the implications of the paper become more important. Paperwork requirements remain an essential component in special education.

Issues over the IEP in informal and formal disagreements are usually the result of something written; for example, a supplemental aid and support or a goal on the IEP that perhaps was not interpreted the same for school staff and parents, or a transition plan that was perceived to be different. These examples abound in every school and district. The actual amount of paper may be reduced—sometimes—but the ramifications of what is written will probably continue to increase in the future.

This is why the methods presented in part II are so important. When the leader of the IEP team follows part II with an understanding of the learning organization and of transformational leadership, that leader will have the basis to enjoy positive interactions between the student, parents, and school staff to discuss, develop together clear ideas, and construct a meaningful IEP that can be implemented at home, in school, and within the community. When there are fewer disagreements or fewer opportunities for misinterpretation, the manifestations of the written words become more understood than if the IEP is constructed without clear outcomes and understanding.

Fear of Regulatory Consequences

This is a real issue. The author has heard too many times from school officials that practices within a school and in special education are in place to first avoid legal consequences followed by what is best for the student. Obviously this is not the intention of the original P.L. 94-142 or the most recent version of IDEA, but it is real and it exists throughout the K–12 system.

There are times change is not a part of the school climate or is not considered because any change may result in a negative consequence, whether from an unsatisfied parent or a state or federal regulatory agency. This fear reduces opportunities for students to maximize achievement because the spirit of the special education rule is lost in the letter of the law. The spirit clearly is to enhance all opportunities for student achievement, not to be restricted by the letter of the law.

The Theory of Missed Opportunities helps IEP teams, schools, and districts to see how change can occur to reduce missed opportunities for student achievement through better IEP team functions and construction of IEPs. By understanding the role of a learning organization and employing a transformational leadership style, the manifestations we often feel plagued by, such as not enough time, too many IEPs, fear of change, and fear of consequences, can be bridged so we can significantly reach out to our students with disabilities.

ANALYSIS

1. How does the application of the Theory of Missed Opportunities affect the operation of IEP teams?
2. Why does a team need to consider transformational leadership as a means to quality improvement?
3. What are you going to do to start an initiative for applying learning organization and transformational leadership into your IEP team leadership style?

EVALUATION

1. Where do you see conflicts between just good enough and greatness in your IEP team structures and your IEPs?
2. What can you do to start an initiative of systemic quality improvement with your IEP teams to produce great IEPs?
3. Where do you see conflict in organizing a change initiative?
4. What can you do about system conflicts?
5. What are the major issues to impede change possibilities?
6. What do you see as possibilities and threats working toward the attributes of a learning organization?

7. What do you see as possibilities and threats working toward the attributes of a transformational leadership style?
8. Do you see natural implementations of a SWOT analysis and double-loop learning to assist your transformational leadership style to address common manifestations of issues affecting the IEP team and the development of the IEP?

Part I Summary

Part I was an attempt to combine some standard theories and practices used in the business community for organizational development to improve organizational effectiveness into a framework to apply to an educational system. Unfortunately there has been a disconnect in the past that business practices do not have a place or purpose in K–12 systems. While this paradigm is changing, progress has been slow and at times carries a dubious characterization.

Most educators have heard stories and examples that in business, management can reject a raw product or inventory and can replace unacceptable performance with better-performing persons. But in education, teachers have no choice in classroom students or curriculum and cannot refuse to educate the "difficult student." This diatribe misconceives the many contributions from the business community to benefit educational systems.

As the reader enters part II, the emphasis on the learning organization and transformational leadership takes on a new meaning in the educational environment, as this environment promotes the difficult concept of change and quality improvement. However, it has been demonstrated that such change and improvement does make for better IEP team function and IEPs for students.

The learning organization and the leadership necessary to harness organizational development are necessary as a prerequisite to part II: how to lead the IEP team and chair the IEP team meeting.

While the business community, particularly management and organization theory, is primarily responsible for the elements of learning organization and for the concept of transformational leadership, it will be up to dedicated educators to transfer the application of learning organization, transformational leadership, and SWOT into an educational arena. Because of the "businesslike" nature of these strategies, it is natural to assume that not all school staff will want to accept these and other documented methods as viable educational tools.

However, as difficult as it may seem to implement a "businesslike" strategy into the educational system, it is imperative that efforts are exerted toward quality improvement. It is quite understood that society is demanding accountability throughout all of the K–12 systems in this country. Taxpayers want to see results of the largest expenditure most state governments make. Educators also know that accountability through test scores, high-stakes testing, and norm-referenced standardized assessments all have significant validity concerns. While most of this is directed toward "regular" education, there are equal concerns regarding special education.

For years expenses related to special education either in staff or supply budgets have not been evaluated to the same degree as staffing and supplies are for regular education. There has been an attitude that because of the federal and state special education law and district fear of consequences for special education services, whatever is requested is granted. Granting under this guise has led to a climate that is misunderstood by the public.

This misunderstanding has been problematic to school districts and will continue to be problematic to all special education services. The public's logic goes like this: "How can we spend so much money in equipment, supplies, and staff to teach kids who will never pay taxes, hold a real job, or make any contribution to our society?"

The misguided logic continues, "If we spent that same amount of money on the kids who will pay taxes, get real jobs, and make contributions to society, how much more can they contribute if money was added to their education, instead of the kids in special education?"

This is why we need great IEP teams and great IEPs. Known practices that have been prevalent in business need to be engaged now. The public has the ability to greatly interfere with success in education, and the public can influence regulation, revenue, perceptions, and attitudes toward special education and the desiring students who have and in the future will benefit from individualized education services to meet unique needs.

Special education cannot rely on test scores, even improved test scores, to demonstrate program effectiveness. The only true assessment of special education effectiveness is to analyze what has happened to previous students receiving special education services after their K–12 experience.

This is risky business, because many students with disabilities are not given a fair shot at employment, postsecondary education, and even independent living arrangements. But there needs to be some assessment for the perusal of the public. This is where great IEPs come into the picture.

Great IEPs utilize student, parent, and school staff input in a collaborative manner to meet outcomes that lead to success for the student as an adult. Students must be able to apply skills that are used at home, in school, and within the community environment. Great IEPs will have a high probability of demonstrating the effectiveness of the IEP and special education services.

It seems clear that just being good enough in special education will not make the cut. Special education can be judged on a variety of components, but the most obvious and the most influential is the IEP team. The team has the sole ability to develop great IEPs. In part II the reader will look at how this can be an ongoing theory-in-use, becoming part of the school's culture and daily norms. The IEP and the success of our special education students are worth every second put into its improvement and every effort to be great.

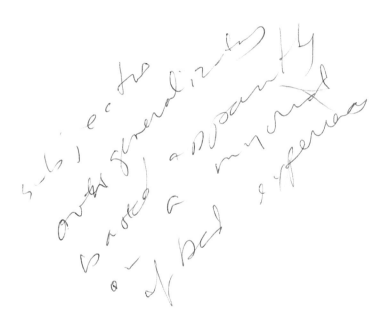

LEADING THE IEP TEAM

INTRODUCTION

Chairing an IEP team meeting is an essential function for the success and the coordination of special education services in any school. Research has demonstrated that when students, parents, teachers, and other school personnel experience a collaborative and productive IEP team meeting, the resulting IEP and the services at school and in the home are usually effective and meet meaningful individual needs of the student.

In many situations IEP team meetings are not effectively or efficiently organized, are not friendly, and team members leave the meeting thinking that their efforts only complied with existing special education law. Sometimes there is animosity, other times members feel too much time was taken to argue or deal only with trivial points that have little to do with acquisition of student skills.

Many times points of law overwhelm the spirit of the IEP and greatly limit the collaborative nature of the IEP meeting. Some IEP team meetings are too long; some may require subsequent future meetings to "finish up." In most cases, parents, teachers, and administrators anticipate the team meetings as a required process to ascertain pertinent paperwork and procedural requirements; most are glad to have the meeting end regardless of the outcome, and a general sense of frustration envelops the IEP process.

However, there have been moments of greatness that evolved from the IEP team meeting. Part II was written to provide a to-the-point guide to facilitate great IEP team meetings and outstanding IEPs. Many readers may read the chapters and say, "I knew this" or "We do this."

But the fact remains, if we already know how to effectively and collaboratively chair an IEP team meeting, there should never be a too-long, frustrating, or unproductive team meeting. Unfortunately, there are. The point is that with an understanding of how to chair the meeting for greatness, the IEP team meeting can be a collaborative, problem-solving, and sharing experience that will result in an IEP that really produces student achievement, parent-school cooperation, and a long-term partnership.

When students, parents, and school staff work together to not only collaborate during the IEP team meeting, but to engage the IEP as a working journey for the student, academic, social, and physical progress can occur at home, in the community, and at school. New student skills become alive and part of the student's repertoire of living skills, in concert with mainstream society.

This all starts to show at the IEP team meeting. If the IEP team is connected, understands its responsibilities, and is focused upon realistic and purposeful outcomes, then great things can happen. Who would argue results such as teachers and parents working together, student engagement, and an IEP that is built upon the strengths of home, school, and community? Furthermore, outstanding IEP team meetings are focused, timesaving, and effective.

Part II will lay out the process in nine short chapters, which when put together will provide the guidelines for chairing an IEP team meeting that all team members will enjoy and contribute to equally. The keys to the successful IEP team meetings are outlined, but two reoccurring themes are present: the parents and the student are key and essential members of the IEP team. Every school employee on any IEP team must know and believe this. The process will quickly fail if students and parents are excluded, underrepresented, or not fully participating in the team meeting structure.

Collaborative and outstanding IEPs facilitate student achievement, build positive school culture, cost less in time and resources, and fulfill the Spirit (spirit) and the letter of the Individuals with Disabilities Education Act (IDEA).

Part II follows a sequential journey through the IEP team meeting process. Chapters 5 through 8 indicate necessary work that goes into the team meeting ahead of time. In many ways these chapters are helping your school and district to look at the culture of the IEP team meeting. Furthermore the leader begins to espouse a norm of welcoming and collaborative team meetings.

Chapters 9 through 11 are topics deeply involved with the actual team meeting, beginning with the agenda, collaboration of outcomes, and creating the IEP goals. The last section of part II, chapters 12 and 13, move a school and district from espousing a collaborative IEP effort to one that really does what the school wants to do. Chapter 12 addresses student, parent, and school staff training and chapter 13 discusses the reasons paperwork demonstrates school commitment toward collaboration. The summary is a list of activities to ensure that the team meeting exceeds expectations.

5

The Right Mindset

KEY POINTS

1. It is essential to develop a positive culture for the IEP team meeting.
2. For over thirty-five years, the IEP framework of federal law has remained basically the same.
3. Great IEPs begin with a commitment to collaborate as a team.

Someone needs to create and define a collaborative and a positive nature to the IEP team meeting; this is probably the reader and the leader. The leader is the host/hostess, the moderator and facilitator of this event. The IEP is the most important educational tool ever created, and the IEP team meeting has huge potential to develop successful education experiences for students. But this will only happen if the leader creates and defines what the attitudes and mindsets are before the IEP team meeting even begins.

The right mindset includes all potential team members, including school administrators, special and regular education teachers, related service personnel, parents, and students (who should be at and participate in every IEP team meeting). The leader's job is to eliminate all preconceived and negative thoughts about past IEP team meetings; the overindulgence of paperwork; and the IEP "war stories" that may be told and retold in the teachers' lounge, in administrative offices, through social networking, and surprisingly at parent support groups and as part of family get-togethers.

The "war stories" say a lot about how people feel about IEP team meetings. They create a negative mindset that will prevail throughout a career or the term of a student's involvement in a school. Recounting a three-day team meeting, or rehashing about the time the parents got really angry, or telling others of the time the family attorney really nailed the special education director, does nothing but perpetuate this negative mindset.

The leader will need to change that, and the following chapters will help you flip this disastrous perception of an IEP team meeting to one that is much shorter, more productive, and more satisfying to all team members. Parents are your ally in this process, not your enemy.

The IEP process starts with an understanding of the original purpose of P.L. 94-142 and all proceeding reauthorizations to provide a free and appropriate education for all students. The team meeting and the IEP have seen little change since 1975.

Educators, and the public, need to remember that before 1975 students with disabilities did not have to be educated in America's public schools. In perspective, the United States put a man on the moon six years before a federal initiative was passed by Congress to ensure that all students have a right to a public education. Since then impressive achievements have been made by students who were able to receive appropriate special education services.

Educators need to recognize that every student has a tremendous potential to learn, that when students with disabilities are integrated into "regular" classrooms, a new dimension is found in our schools and all students can prosper. The increase of society's acceptance of individuals with disabilities appears related to inclusion in our schools.

Furthermore, students, teachers, and parents need to believe that the IEP team process can be a valuable and fulfilling experience that incorporates teacher expertise and creativity and can build a real connectedness between students, parents, and teachers. This is the mindset that will need to start developing with the IEP teams.

This mindset will not happen overnight, but over time if the leader remains committed to a collaborative premise, is consistent in the approach to chairing meetings, and highlights the equal roles of team members including parents and students, great IEPs will follow.

The IEP team meeting is the most important event in a student's educational life. The IEP is the most important educational tool in a student's educational experience. Treat this as the most significant educational event for each student and expect others to ascribe to this premise; this will create a new and thoughtful mindset.

ANALYSIS

1. How can you create a model for others for great IEPs?
2. Why is it important for teachers, students, and parents to work together?
3. What can you do to help others build positive mindsets?

EVALUATION

1. Were you able to express your enthusiasm for the IEP team meeting?
2. Did you talk to team members about the positive and collaborative nature of the IEP team meeting?
3. Did you assess the prevailing culture and norm of your school and district on issues surrounding the IEP team process?
4. Did you check your own perspectives and understanding of the IEP team process?

6

The Invitation

KEY POINTS

1. IEP team members, especially students and parents, need to feel welcome attending the IEP team meeting.
2. Personalize the notice to parents and invite the student in a sincere manner.
3. Most notices of team meetings are unwelcoming.

Sometimes the author receives an invitation to an event in which the envelope has my name and address in a very nice, scrolled, handwritten format; there is an extra piece of tissue paper in the folded invitation card; and the ink is gold. Other times the author receives an invitation on the back of a postcard that is computer generated, and my name is misspelled.

The author tends to treat the two invitations very differently: for one the author always has hopes of being invited to the White House (never has happened), and for one the author usually dumps it in a nearby trash can. While the cost to the senders is not significantly different, the results of the effort that went into each make a greatly different impression.

Look at the Notice of an IEP Team Meeting form used by your school district. Sure, the form letter has all the legal and required bits of information, but put yourself in the role of the receiver of this notice. Does this invitation make one feel welcome, an event someone would like to attend, something to look forward to? It should, but rarely does it have this effect, and it's actually less welcoming than the computer-generated postcard with my name spelled wrong.

This is the start of the process that parents taste well before the IEP team meeting. The state requires the notice to include information such as date,

75

time, and place. There are lists of who is being invited and sometimes what their roles are in the IEP team meeting, and in smaller print a statement that the meeting can be changed if the time does not work for parents.

Welcoming—NO; motivating—NO; an idea of what parents are supposed to bring, do, or say—NO; something to look forward to, even if it is about their child—NO; something ground-shakingly important—NO; legal and compliant—YES. Welcome to the IEP team! What a way for parents to start or even continue this most important of all meetings in which the educational program or school placement is being determined for their child and your student.

Oh, and of course, the parents and students are equal partners in this effort? It doesn't happen.

It is obviously not possible to send a gold-inked invitation with tissue paper in a scrolled and beautifully handcrafted envelope with names spelled correctly to announce an IEP team meeting. You have to send the official Notice of an IEP Team Meeting form—for no reason other than to be compliant with state and federal law; however, you can

1. Add a sticky note on the official form to say you are looking forward to Johnny's IEP team meeting and seeing the parents again, or
2. Send a handwritten or typed letter welcoming the parents to the school and the meeting and outline a few ideas that may come up at the meeting, or
3. Send along some ideas of what information would be important for school personnel to hear, ideas for educational outcomes (goals), and observations parents have made since the last meeting. See *Hopes and Dreams: An IEP Guide for Parents with Children with Autism Spectrum Disorder* (Lentz, 2004) for a good method for parents to equally and meaningfully participate in the IEP team meetings, even if the student does not have an autism spectrum disorder.

Make the invitation welcoming; make it real. The leader will want to have the parents receive this notice and say, "Good, I have some ideas to share and I am interested in hearing what ideas the teachers have. I'm looking forward to this time so we can work together to help John learn some pretty important stuff. It will also be good to see some of John's teachers again."

ANALYSIS

1. How can you make the notice of an IEP team meeting welcoming?
2. Why is it important to personalize the notice of a team meeting?
3. What can you do to make the next team meeting more inviting?

EVALUATION

1. Did you include something personal with the formal notice of an IEP team meeting?
2. Does your district's official notice of an IEP team meeting include all of the required components according to your state's law, including who was invited; role each invited member has; time and date of the team meeting; and a notice that the time and date can be changed to meet the needs of the parents or other external (advocate, relative, or others at the request of the parents) persons?
3. Do you feel your personal note was welcoming, motivating, and based upon a collaborative effort to develop or monitor an outstanding education plan for the student?
4. Do the parents know what is expected of them before and during the team meeting?

7

The Preparation for the IEP Team Meeting

KEY POINTS

1. Teachers and school staff must have evaluations completed when necessary.
2. Parent preparation is based upon parents knowing what is expected of them before and during the IEP team meeting.
3. Student preparation is just being fair to the student.

Preparation for an IEP team meeting is critical, for the leader, school staff, and the parents and student. We will briefly talk about the IEP team leader, teachers, and parents and students separately.

IEP TEAM LEADER PREPARATION

Never think that all the leader needs to do is walk into the conference room or any other extraordinarily small place where the team meeting will be held, without any idea of what to expect. Also never assume that teachers, student, and parents know what is expected of them during the team meeting—a recipe for everything not good!

Connect with all appropriate teachers, related service personnel, and administrators (this will also make the leader look good!) to make sure that they have the date and time on their schedule. Reinforce that they need to attend—on time, or come a little early for some pleasantries with the student and parents. If any evaluations are necessary, ensure that they are completed and in written form.

It is always good for school staff to have some educational ideas to present dealing with specific academic, behavioral, social, or physical issues. The leader never wants to have IEP goals already written for the parents to sign, just ideas made from observations, evaluations, and direct work with the student.

Review past IEPs, evaluations, placement, and current status of active goals from the present IEP before the team meeting. Have a solid idea of how Jane is doing in all areas and use your expertise to analyze the education services, placement, related services, and supplemental aids and supports. Know how well the school is doing to prepare Johnny for success.

It may be a good idea to contact the parents by phone or e-mail and ask if they have any concerns or questions about the forthcoming IEP team meeting. An e-mail sent three days before can work very nicely; this extends the welcome and paints a very progressive picture of the leader and the district. This can also be a good time to reinforce the parents' preparation process discussed in a following section in this chapter.

Lastly prepare an agenda. Chapter 9 will guide this exercise. It is important to know that while there is a standard agenda, each IEP should have variations to the standard simply due to the unique needs each student and family brings to the table. Some examples of typical variations that require adjustments to the agenda are a future transition from elementary to middle or middle to high school, observed increase in challenging behaviors, and changing conditions at home or at school. Make adjustments and any additions prior to the actual meeting.

The leader can also share the agenda with IEP team members, including the student and parents, so each will have an idea of the order and topics to be discussed. This will not only save a lot of time, but you will be organized and it will show. Parents can, and want to be, indisputably proud of their school. It is the little things, like a prepared and shared agenda, that make a big difference.

SCHOOL STAFF PREPARATION

The school staff must come to the IEP team meeting with documentation, evaluations as appropriate, and ideas. For the school staff to attend while not being fully prepared is simply unacceptable. The author has heard over and over that an evaluation is not finished because "It took so much longer to complete than expected" or "I didn't have time to get it written up." These statements are not good enough, especially when parents often take time off from work or are leaving other children at home to attend the team meeting, and the student is missing instructional time in school.

At minimum, school staff need written evaluations and assessments (copies for the parents is always a great idea—"the little things"); well-thought-out ideas for educational strategies and techniques; a general sense of program outcomes or goals; and a thought-out presentation of the student's current status, achievements, and areas of concern.

Evaluations are always an important part of the teacher and specialist's report. A short explanation of the tests used and the reasons for administering a specific assessment help staff and parents understand the nature and scope of the evaluation.

The leader's job is to check with appropriate teachers and staff to make sure they are prepared and have all necessary components on-hand. This is a "pay now or pay much more later" situation. Paying later is embarrassing and does not reflect well on the IEP team, the school staff, or the school, and most important does not fulfill the spirit of the special education law. The IEP team leader will have many IEP teams in the school, but the leader will absolutely minimize the workload by ensuring in the beginning that school staff is prepared and the family contacted before the team meeting, rather than later when things go badly.

PARENT PREPARATION

Guide parents before the IEP team meeting!!! Most parents are uncomfortable and do not know what their role really is during the meeting. Assist them. Help parents to be prepared by asking them to do the following (see *Hopes and Dreams*, Lentz):

1. List all the new skills Jane has learned and where she is using the skills.
2. List emerging skills, as these are skills you will want to focus on for goals on the IEP.
3. List interests that Jane has outside of school; teachers will appreciate this information, and interests are a wonderful teaching tool.
4. List the things that parents see that will make a difference in the quality of life for Johnny and the family.
5. List the ideas that parents have to share learning outcomes between school, home, and the community.

If we are asking Jane to work hard and learn new skills, it is incumbent upon the school to make sure that new skills are applicable and valuable in the home, school, and community environments. See the Test of Utility described in chapter 2. The efforts to teach the skills must be carried out in all environments. The information from the parents and student becomes very important. This outline of information from parents actually forms the basis for a parents' assessment.

Most evaluations and assessments consist of four reporting sections: strengths, areas of need, prognosis, and program recommendations. The parents' assessment outline does this: learned skills are assessment strengths, emerging skills are areas for improvement or skills to be worked on, outcomes for quality of life are the prognoses, and collaborations with school are program recommendations.

Parents will need support to complete this assessment, and you can do this with a couple of contacts prior to the IEP team meeting and with the parent training discussed in chapter 12. Assistance will be most appreciated by parents to help them know what information to present and how to present it. The leader will include in the prepared agenda a time at the beginning or toward the end of the discipline evaluation reports for parents to share their important information. The leader can ask the parents if they have a preference.

Sometimes parents like to report early to share the information before the meeting moves into the school reports and evaluations. Some parents may prefer to do their presentation after they have heard the reports and findings to augment their information and to shed a different light on some areas. Honor the parent wishes; the leader's job is to make this a welcoming meeting and help parents to be equal partners in the IEP process.

STUDENT PREPARATION

The author has seen too many times the student being invited to their IEP team meeting only to sit, not participate or "act out." This is just not fair. The author has also seen students practice in a learning situation participating in an IEP team meeting, asking questions, and providing input. The author has also seen students chair their own meeting.

With some practice and instruction of expectations and roles people play at these meetings, many students become engaged and active in very appropriate ways. Far too often, though, the student is unprepared and becomes either a passive participant or disruptive, wanting out in the worst way.

This becomes another "pay now or really pay later" situation. The efforts to instruct and practice a team meeting with the student will be a time-consuming effort in the beginning, but as time goes on, imagine the possibilities as students become active participants. To ask a student to attend a team meeting without any supports or knowing what the expectation and procedures are is just not fair and builds a pretty poor attitude toward the IEP process.

The student, with necessary support, may follow the outline used by the parents. School staff can assist and offer some ideas. Students can and should provide their own perception of school achievement and progress and then provide ideas to make their lives more valuable and meaningful. See appendix B.

Sometimes, either due to cognitive or behavioral abilities, the student may find the IEP team meeting too overwhelming or produce hypersensitivity to the construct of this event. The chairperson of the meeting, in concert with parents, should decide how much of the meeting the student should attend and to what degree. Some parents report that they have a hard time focusing on the content of the meeting when they are concerned about or dealing with behavioral responses from the student.

Obviously the student should have sufficient learning opportunities to participate as a member of the team, but a basic "risk vs. benefit" analysis should be considered to ensure that parents and school staff are able to conduct business. If the student is interfering with this process, the team may decide that the student should attend for short periods of time or at different times in the meeting agenda.

This may be a difficult decision due to the federal and state law affecting special education and the desire for the student to participate in the team meeting, but if the student is not adequately prepared for this event, commonsense decisions may become necessary.

In most cases, the student should be able to sincerely express interests and hopes for the future and discuss with school personnel and parents what education avenues are necessary for future aspirations. Even for young students, knowing their interests and their hopes will build dreams and is motivating.

When future student aspirations change over time, new interests are always presented for school and home to build new educational pathways. New interests almost always provide new motivations, experiences, and emerging skills that need to be shared with the IEP team so teaching emphasis can also change to reflect these new opportunities.

ANALYSIS

1. How will you assess the degree of preparation by school staff prior to an IEP team meeting?
2. Why is parent preparation important; is it easier when parents are not prepared?
3. Why is student preparation important; what happens if students are not prepared?

4. How will you assist students in your school to be prepared for their own IEP team meeting?

EVALUATION

1. Did you contact IEP team members prior to the IEP team meeting?
2. Were all IEP team members prepared for the team meeting before the scheduled IEP team meeting?
3. Were the parents contacted and assessed for their level of preparedness?
4. Did parents complete the parents' assessment?
5. Was the student assisted to understand the context of the team meeting?
6. Did the student have ideas and present interest and future aspirations?
7. Did you feel prepared for the IEP team meeting? Did you review current and past IEPs and evaluations? Did you have a basic understanding of current educational performance? Were you aware of any transitions or changing conditions facing the student?

8

The Ground Rules for School Staff

KEY POINTS

1. The IEP team meeting needs to be professionally yet personally conducted.
2. Ground rules help parents and school staff interface and collaborate.
3. Ground rules help provide an equal level of participation.

When the time comes for the IEP team meeting, do not assume anything and always treat everyone the same. Courtesy, even with historically contentious parents, advocates, and attorneys, goes far in creating a positive culture for the team meeting. This will take the edge off and is just nice to do. Parents and other external persons make a special effort to attend the team meetings, often at convenient times for school personnel. Extend an appreciation to the parents with the school being welcoming and school staff attending on time.

Obviously the team always introduce ourselves, but so many times the author has heard team members introduce themselves by saying, "I'm Joe," assuming all attending would know Joe is the adapted physical education teacher. Instead try, "I'm Joe Green. I am the adapted physical education teacher and I see Johnny during third hour in an inclusive P.E. class."

It works best when the school staff are present for the entire meeting (that's why it is important to chair the meeting effectively, so people do not need to leave). It is so disruptive and rude when personnel come into the meeting after it starts and after introductions are made. The leader may need to demand that people arrive on time and stay! The author often wondered, as a parent, who the "new people" were when persons came into the meetings after introductions. Also it sends the wrong message to parents when a teacher may have to give her report first so she can leave and do something much more important than participate in "my child's IEP meeting." These are little things that have a huge impact upon the perception of you and your school.

It is also rude when everyone sits down for the IEP team meeting and the school staff comes in with the crusty coffee mug, or with a soda can, or with a refreshing bottle of cold water, even worse arriving with the last bite of a baloney sandwich and a Glad bag. No more; no eating during an IEP team meeting. It's okay to bring in a soda, water, or one refreshment for themselves, *only* if the same is made available to the parents and student.

It is strongly recommended that food and coffee not be placed on the conference table or even in the room being used. The team is there to work efficiently and effectively. With a temptation of refreshments, someone will always be up getting more coffee or food. This distracts from the meeting and disrupts the process. The idea is to have shorter but meaningful meetings; do not drag it out by making it a "social engagement or lunch."

As chair, the leader will need to do a visual check before the meeting starts and even before people sit down. Have the parents and the school staff positioned in a way that does not separate parents or the student from the rest of the team, which creates an atmosphere of all being equal. The goal is to have a professional yet personal meeting to develop very important program delivery options for a student. Everyone is busy—parents and teachers have other things to do, so get to work in a courteous, friendly, focused team meeting.

More will be said later, but instruct the school staff to report on actual findings and statements that are factual. Too many times, in an effort to be comforting and nice, school staff will use words such as, "He's really smart." or "She's real good in my class." These comments are recognized by parents as weak and meaningless. So leave them alone.

Parents want to hear what is actual and factual, even if the teacher perceives the facts as disheartening; the actual is always appreciated by the parents. Parents want a clear and accurate picture, not a glossy under- or overrepresentation of their child's true status in school, even when it may be hard for a teacher to communicate the clear picture.

ANALYSIS

1. How do you prepare for current IEP team meetings? Are they focused and to the point?
2. Why is it important to have ground rules? What is the chance such rules make the IEP team meeting overly formal and too businesslike?

3. What can you do differently to set the team meeting to be productive and friendly?

EVALUATION

1. Are teachers and specialists familiar with the "ground rules"?
2. Do teachers and specialists demonstrate the "ground rules"?
3. Did you encourage the use of the "ground rules"?
4. Did you create an environment conducive to a meaningful yet personal interaction?

9

The Agenda

KEY POINTS

1. Organize the flow of the IEP team meeting so all important information is presented and substantive education decisions can be made.
2. Utilize the knowledge from parents and students to the greatest degree possible.
3. Make team-oriented plans for the IEP at the meeting.

We said in chapter 7 that the agenda for any IEP team meeting should be adjusted to meet the individual needs of the student, parent, or educational situation; there is a basic boilerplate that should be used. Regardless if the team meeting is to determine special education eligibility, placement, three-year IEP, annual review, or a special meeting to discuss specific components of the IEP, the following agenda will serve most situations well.

1. Begin with a welcome statement that includes the purpose of the meeting, the general agenda of the meeting, the general outcome of the meeting, and who will chair the meeting. A sample could be, "Welcome to Johnny's annual review of his IEP. As you know, this is the second review of his three-year IEP, and Johnny seems to be making good progress since we met last year.

   "Today we will hear from Johnny and then Mr. and Mrs. Johnson about how things are going at home, school, and in the community, and then Johnny's teachers will each give us an update of what is going on in the classroom and other environments at school. At the end of this meeting we should be able to determine if we need to make any changes with

Johnny's IEP goals, related services, and supplemental aids and supports. If at any time anyone has a question, please feel free to ask, and thank you for your participation. Remember every concept, idea, and experience is important, and we will discuss all recommendations. Let's get started."

2. The second item on the agenda should be a statement from the student, after the student has had an opportunity to practice and has had supports to determine what he or she will be saying. The student can say what his or her hopes and aspirations are, what is important to the student, and what the student would like to learn to meet personal outcomes.

   Sometimes it may be appropriate for the parents to speak on behalf of the student when the student has significant communication needs, but generally there are functional modalities of communication that convey the goals and outcomes as seen by the student.

3. The student's comments are then followed by the parents' information outlined by the aforementioned parent preparation guidelines. Parents should indicate new skills observed at home and during involvements with others and in the community, emerging skills they are noticing during naturally occurring activities, outcomes that will improve the quality of life for the family and the child, and then ideas to coordinate efforts between the school, home, and community.

   This is important information and must be treated as equally important as any other discipline evaluation. Parents who do present a parents' assessment have put a tremendous amount of work into their observations and their analysis of their child's ability to function at home, with others, and around town; their information is generally very honest and realistic. In fact, many IEP team members from the school say this information should guide the foundation of the entire IEP process.

   See what process your district uses to teach or prepare parents before the IEP to help parents prepare for the IEP team process and to assist parents to work collaboratively with teachers and the school.

   There may not be a process, and you will want to look into a training program for parents. See chapter 12 on parent training. Research clearly indicates that when parents are knowledgeable of the team process and have training to be equal partners, IEP team meetings take less time and center on real student needs that are addressed at home, school, and in the community.

4. The next agenda item is the reports from the school team members. The order should usually start with the main teacher or the special education teacher. The reports should essentially follow the same procedure used by the parents: strengths or recently learned skills; areas for improvement or emerging skills—usually active goals from the IEP and

the status of each; the desired outcomes of the learning process; and recommendations for generalization of skills within the school and suggestions for active involvement at home and in the community.

Each specialized service area, such as speech and occupational therapy, positive behavior intervention, resources, and so on, needs to be covered. After each report, the chair needs to look at the parents and other team members and ask, "Are there any questions? Do you have ideas you would like to share? Are there things you have noticed at home or in your classrooms pertaining to this report?" If so, this does prepare the team for discussions later on developing the educational program; if not, the chair will introduce the next reporter.

It is essential that the chair jots some notes of the summary and key points made in the evaluation. This information will be used to summarize the reports before the team engages in the decision-making process: step #5.

5. The chair of this IEP team meeting then should summarize the strengths and needs, the recommendations and desired outcomes. For example, at an IEP team meeting for a middle school boy, Jack, with an autism spectrum disorder: "From listening to Jack, his parents, and the various reports, what I have consistently heard is the need for Jack to improve initiating communication needs to others, learn how to appropriately handle noise and commotion in large groups, and to develop comprehension skills to follow written directions and reading assignments. I also have heard that by using a social story, Jack seems to understand changes in his routines, and a visual schedule for his entire school day could be helpful. These are things I think we will want to keep in mind as we discuss goals and supports for Jack. Does anyone have anything else, or do you have other ideas before we discuss the goals?"

6. The chair then will need to gather consensus of the outcomes and coordinate a team discussion of using the outcomes to formulate goals that will be included or modify goals on the IEP. This is a team decision, not a preconceived action.

Sometimes the chair can start the discussion on goals by saying, "It seems like Jack could benefit from goals dealing with initiating expressive communication, demonstrating appropriate social skills across environments, and comprehending written materials. What do you think?"

All reports, including those from the parents and student, are to be equally considered in this decision. Sometimes there is discussion of whether the outcomes seen by the parents or student really fit into the scope of school responsibility. At times school administrators and teachers do not want to include things such as making friends at the playground, toilet skills, or getting a part-time job as an educational construct.

The key is that almost everything can be tied into a framework of education. While making friends at a community playground may be a stretch regarding educational responsibility, school outcomes sure come into play when supports are provided to teach appropriate peer interactions during P.E. classes, lunchtime, and recess. Toileting occurs at school and is then inherently a school-related responsibility.

Likewise, getting a part-time job outside of the school day does fit into transition planning requirements, and supports can easily be provided within a context of skills necessary to have a job—such as money skills, vocational training, and social skill development. In essence everything necessary to ensure success from K–12 to adult living can be seen as having an educational responsibility and application.

7. After the goals have been agreed to and understood by the IEP team members, the next agenda item will be a discussion of the appropriateness and requirements for related services. Remember that the team, not individuals, makes the decision if any and which specific related services are appropriate for the student. The team also agrees on the frequency and location provided by the related service.

Typical related services include speech, physical, or occupational therapy; counseling; nursing; special transportation needs; social work and case management services; 1:1 services; psychological services; visual and auditory assistance; and orientation and mobility.

The optimum degree of services is the key to related services, not to settle for the cheapest to the district, or the most in the minds of parents. It simply comes down to what will best get the job done and allow the student to maintain as normal a school day as possible.

The author remembers a conflictive situation after a speech and language therapist recommended that the student receive speech therapy in a small group. The parents were dead set against this recommendation, as they wanted to have more 1:1 time with the speech therapist. Trouble was brewing, until the speech therapist was asked why she was recommending that speech services be offered in a small group.

She responded that at the last meeting, the parents wanted the student to be able to engage in conversational activities with peers, and she and the student had worked hard to learn words and role-play in situations. The therapist felt now was the time to use those skills learned in a contrived environment in a real social situation. The parents were concerned that their child did not have a strong enough vocabulary and comprehension to do that.

However, the speech therapist said that she would be evaluating the individuals in the group but felt that the communication interactions with peers would reinforce any 1:1 learning that could take place in her office. The parents understood, and the small group communication therapy worked out very successfully for the student.

8. Once related services are agreed upon, the chair will need to lead a discussion of supports necessary to ensure success. These areas are called supplemental aids and supports, program modifications, and accommodations. These services are across the board and most times are uniquely defined by the needs of the student.

   Examples could include extra time on tests, directions read to the student, large-print reading materials, visual schedules, modified curriculum, teacher training, and consultation, to name a few. This cannot be done until the team has adequately reviewed and consents to the IEP goal status and related services, and all team members have a solid understanding of current performance (present levels of academic functioning) from the provided reports.

   Several examples of supplemental aids and supports that have been used include limiting the student from long exposure in the sun without sunblock due to medications taken by the student; use of visual schedules throughout the school day; because of seizures, the student should not be outside on hot and humid days; social and behavioral cue cards for known difficult situations; a ruler carried by the child to mark his place with reading material; seating arranged to block sun glare on the whiteboard; toilet schedule; times for large muscle group use; walking in the hallway to relieve stress and feeling of being overwhelmed; and practicing good peer-interaction conversational skills. While these supports do not reach the formality of a long-term goal, they are perhaps, in certain cases, as or more important than the goals presented on the IEP.

9. There are a number of additional items that may apply to a student's IEP, such as the ability to participate in statewide testing or if the team decides that the student should participate in an alternative state assessment, extended school year, and any other verification of special education eligibility.

10. The chair should conclude the meeting by asking if there is any other information team members wish to present. Then provide a quick summary of the team meeting and indicate any follow-up actions necessary: "Well, this ends Jack's IEP team meeting; however, before we leave does anyone wish to make any other comments, or are there issues that were not covered or addressed that may be important to include either in the discussion or the IEP?"

The chair can summarize by saying, "I will have this IEP modified in the next two weeks and distributed to all team members. Remember we can make changes to the goals and other parts of the IEP, so if there is anything amiss or that we need to discuss further, please let me know and I will schedule another meeting."

11. Thank everyone for attending and treat this IEP team meeting like it is the only team meeting the school staff ever needs to attend; it is for the parents and the student.

The standard agenda should look like:

1. Welcome
2. Student-shared information
3. Parent-shared information
4. School staff-shared information by discipline
5. Summary of shared information (strengths, needs, recommendations)
6. Decision making for consensus of goals on or for IEP
7. Decision making for related services
8. Decision making for supplemental aids and supports
9. Decision making for extended school year and testing
10. Additional information or comments
11. Adjourn and thank you

ANALYSIS

1. How does your school typically conduct the IEP team meeting?
2. Why is it important to follow a structured but individualized agenda that is developed ahead of time for each student?
3. What can you do differently preparing for the next IEP team meeting?

EVALUATION

1. Was the agenda prepared ahead of time and shared with the IEP team members?
2. Was the agenda specifically developed for the individual student?
3. Did you welcome everyone to the meeting and do introductions?
4. Was the student able to express things that were important to him or her?

5. Were the parents engaged, and did they present important information to the team?
6. Were the reports from school staff clear and concise?
7. Were reports from assessments and evaluations understandable, and reasons presented as to why a particular test was administered without acronyms and esoteric data and statements?
8. Were team members able to ask questions and feel free to make comments about evaluations and recommendations?
9. Were discussions student focused?
10. Did you summarize the reports and evaluations in a manner that was facilitative to discussions about development of goals and supplemental aids and supports?
11. Did team members appear to be satisfied with the results of the team meeting?
12. Did the team meeting last less than ninety minutes?

10

Collaboration of Outcomes

KEY POINTS

1. Developing collaborative outcomes is the keystone to outstanding IEPs.
2. Student, parents, and school staff need to be actively and equally involved.
3. Outcomes must be directly relevant and meaningful to a student's future life.

As indicated in the previous chapter, the outcomes or the goals on the student's IEP are an agreed-upon plan to deal with the most important educational issues for each student. This is the most crucial aspect of the IEP. The goals drive everything else, such as related services, supplemental aids, and supports. Many times problems arise from the goals not being agreed upon by parents and teachers; this can and will cause significant problems.

In order for goals to be consistently agreed upon, parents, students, and the school staff need to work from a model that encourages collaboration, respect, and understanding. This only happens when parents are comfortable as an IEP team member, equally participate, and contribute to the information sharing and decision-making processes during the team meeting. This is not an easy role for parents in this environment.

Many parents do not know the laws and the IEP process like school officials and school personnel do. This entire process is as foreign to most parents as it would be for teachers to do the parents' jobs without much vocational background. The school staff will need to provide assistance and even some basic parent training so parents can be equal partners.

Being equal partners means that parents need to know what to report to the team, how to suggest goals for outcomes, and relate family and community outcomes to the IEP team. Parents as equal partners must also understand the presented information from school evaluations and progress reporting, appreciate the need to generalize learned and nearly learned skills across environments, and to feel comfortable during the IEP team meeting.

During the discussion of goals after the reports and evaluations during most IEP team meetings, the team chair should ask the team, including the parents, what are the most necessary educational outcomes for the student at this time. Usually parents have good ideas, even though they may appear not to easily fit into a clear-cut educational paradigm.

Using some ingenuity and the supplemental aids and supports discussed in the next chapter, it is possible to include parent outcomes that are readily pertinent to the educational process. Recommendations that are brought forth by school personnel are likewise important. It will be the team chair that should be responsible for the coordination and synthesis of various goal ideas into a reasonable number and content of goals that should be included in the student's IEP.

The team chair must be able to recognize the importance of each recommendation and effectively blend similar ideas together. It is also important for the chair to recognize the importance of all recommendations for outcomes and goals. No one is going to suggest goals that they do not believe are important, or do not have meaning.

Therefore the team leader cannot discredit important ideas by not addressing each concept. The leader must be able to transcribe good ideas into goals, and if good ideas are not to be goals, then include appropriate recommendations as supplemental aids and supports or include these ideas at a later time.

Almost every outcome will have an educational component; therefore, outcomes can be molded into the IEP either in the form of an annual goal, or addressed by a related service, or added to supplemental aids and supports. In some school districts IEP goals are aligned directly with applicable state standards. Accommodating an outcome relating to a social skill, or an activity of daily living such as toileting, or a behavioral strategy may be difficult when the emphasis is heavily placed upon standards.

However, using teacher creativity and the supplemental aids and supports, individual student needs can be adequately addressed in the student's IEP. I have seen toileting skills written as a science (biology) goal and behavior self-regulation as a social studies standard goal.

STUDENT INPUT

Many students have learned how to participate in their own IEP team meeting, and students have chaired the IEP team meeting. This usually occurs after the student has had training and practice in doing so. See appendix B. However, the critical factor is students need to be able to express what is most important for them. Students should be asked to respond to or to make statements about their interests, what they would like to learn, and what their future hopes and dreams are.

The author recalls a young student saying he likes trucks; this is okay. The teachers used trucks teaching reading and math skills, and the young man made great progress. As the student became older, other interests emerged. We, as school officials, need to value the current interests of students and use the information to make the educational process meaningful and valuable.

With experiences and exposure to new activities and explorations of new subjects, students who had been involved in the IEP team meetings now have an appreciation of the process and can participate with a higher degree of involvement. In middle and high school, students should be thinking about their adult years, where they would like to live, what they would like to do, what kind of jobs they would enjoy, what interest they may have in postsecondary education, and what students need to know and do in order to pursue what, at that particular time, they think are reasonable and appropriate options.

Countless times it is heard that a student will say he or she wants to be a fireman or a pilot or an army general. While we cannot say a student could not do any of these noble jobs, the two important concepts are (a) what are the current interests of the student and (b) where is the student now and what skills does the student think he or she will need to learn to become what the student wants at this time.

If a student wants to be a fireman, we should be asking or explaining what a fireman needs to learn to be a fireman and use this information as part of his educational experiences. It is very upsetting when a student says, "I want to be a doctor," and members of the IEP team laugh and snicker at the idea. These are valid thoughts at this time, and we need to use this interest to pique new experiences and exposures. We need to listen very carefully to what students tell us and nurture their hopes and dreams to expand their skill repertoire.

PARENT INPUT

Parents may need to be encouraged and, if necessary, taught to present information to the IEP team in the following areas: (a) learned skills; (b) emerging skills; (c) outcomes that significantly impact home and community (these outcomes are rarely not relevant to an educational setting); and (d) recommendations for school and home collaboration.

Learned skills are those activities that the student has recently learned and can apply the skills to naturally occurring tasks and events. Note: If learned skills do not apply to any use in real life, we need to ask why we have taught such skills. Learned and applied skills are a reason to celebrate!

Emerging skills are important because these are the skills that the student either has indicated are interesting or sees as important for independence. Emerging skills are those activities in which the student is starting to engage learning.

These skills may take the form of trying new things, expanding upon a previously learned skill, or attempting further mastery. This is where the IEP team needs to focus on goal development. The curriculum mandates certain alignment to state requirements, but ingenuity and creativeness can be used to blend these important emerging skills to roughly align with state standards.

Outcomes are those dreams parents bring to the IEP team table that are important for the quality and integration of home and community life. Outcomes from parents and from other members of the IEP team begin the goal-setting requirements of the IEP. Most of the time the outcomes presented by parents are applicable to school and the IEP process. Most parents see reasonable outcomes and understand partialization toward outcomes.

Usually parents do present outcomes that affect home life, interactions of the child with other people (familiar and strangers), and integration into the local community. What is important is these are environments that the school personnel rarely see, and these environments are where skills need to be applied.

The IEP team cannot ignore home, community, and other people outside of the school environment. If skills taught at school do not have use at home, with people outside of the school, or during community events and activities; these skills should have little importance in school and on the IEP! Listen carefully to parents; they usually have a very knowledgeable and rational perspective.

There are times when parents or advocates do have outcomes that are considered to be outside the realm of possibility. One grandmother, the student's guardian, wanted her seventeen-year-old with a moderate cognitive disability to go to college. The team respectfully discussed entrance requirements and the type of high school diploma the student would earn (Basic Skills) that would eliminate a four-year college admission. The team thought of other alternatives such as a technical college and educational opportunities as an adult in the community. Within a short amount of time, the team made plans for the student to take some avocational classes at the two-year college.

Collaboration between home and school is critical. Since skills are to be used and applied in home and school environments, understanding how to integrate the learning process enhances the ability of the student to not only learn the skill, but to practice and use these emerging skills in real life. As the student sees value to learning the skill, learning accelerates and becomes meaningful.

Value of learning is promoted by attempts to apply emerging skills in all environments and situations. With genuine collaboration parents and teachers have a common ground to teach, to share success and difficulties, and report progress. Collaboration at this level makes the IEP team work in the spirit it was originally intended, and collaboration leads to the purposeful acquisition of important life skills for the child and student.

PARENT EVALUATION

All disciplines, such as speech and occupational therapist, school psychologist, and reading specialist, should report findings of evaluative procedures at IEP team meetings. When parents report following the outline of the parents' assessment of learned skills, emerging skills, outcomes, and recommendations for school-home collaboration, parents are also presenting evaluation results.

The parents' evaluation needs to carry the same weight as any other discipline evaluation. Much of the parents' evaluation will be based upon observation; these data provide a complete picture of the student—home, school, and community. The chair of the IEP team must convey the importance of parent information to the entire IEP team.

TEAM COLLABORATION

Collaboration of outcomes begins when all IEP team members share relevant data and recommendations. When all team members have a clear understanding of the recommendations and outcomes, the chair of the IEP team then facilitates the team to organize and create meaningful and purposeful IEP goals. This is discussed in the next chapter. However, to adequately generate realistic goals that will lead to application of learned skills across all environments, all members must contribute and participate in a collaborative manner as partners in the effort to build capacity for each student.

ANALYSIS

1. How do evaluation recommendations become meaningful goals?
2. Why is it important to consider not only school, but also parent information for collaborative IEP team meetings and IEPs?

3. What will you do differently to start building toward a collaborative IEP?

EVALUATION

1. Did the student present ideas and hopes for the future?
2. Did team members value the input from the student?
3. Did the parents participate in the discussion of educational outcomes?
4. Were recommendations from all team members treated in a respectful manner?
5. Did the discussions surrounding decision making have equal input from all team members?
6. Were discussions collaborative? Team members working toward similar outcomes?

11

The Summary: IEP Goals

KEY POINTS

1. Parent and teacher dissatisfaction usually occurs during the development of IEP goals.
2. Goals cannot be predetermined prior to the IEP team meeting.
3. Sharing of factual and purposeful information is the key for outstanding IEP goals.

There are too many times during IEP team meetings that prepared goals are brought to the IEP team meeting by school personnel. Goals that are predetermined—brought to the IEP team meeting by school personnel without any consideration for such goals to be discussed and coordinated with other information—destroy the team function. This is what brings trouble to the IEP team and creates animosity and parent dissatisfaction.

It is clearly intended by P.L. 94-142 and every revision since 1975 that the IEP goals were to be decided at the IEP team meeting and only after the team had adequate information to make this important decision—what to teach the student to ensure that the student will be as successful as possible as an adult. But through the years paperwork has greatly increased, time has become more constrained, and more students are receiving special education than ever considered back in 1975.

Preparing goals ahead of time was a cure to the problems of paperwork, time, and too many special education students. Parents either just accepted the recommendations of the school professionals or argued and disagreed with the plan.

The result of such efforts created a well-defined chasm between school and parents. Once parent disagreements began, these disagreements often continued through all future team meetings. Once parents passively accepted the recommendations of the school professionals, parents became increasingly disengaged and nonparticipatory. These chasms do not lead toward the potential success of the student.

Parents need to understand they are equal members of the team and their perspective is essential to the adequacy of the resulting IEP. Prepared goals do not lead to this end and in fact do little to reduce paperwork and time.

IEP goal development needs to be discussed at the IEP team meeting and only after everyone has presented information and recommendations. Because short-term objectives are no longer required for most IEPs, goals have an estimated time frame for one to three school years to be mastered. Therefore goals tend to be rather fluid and wide rather than specific.

The discussion of goals must occur to develop specific learning needs in generalized home, school, and community environments. The discussion to create such outcomes is the crux of the IEP process and can be an enjoyable and sharing experience for IEP team members. Of course state mandates apply, but the real work is the collaboration and coordination between all team members toward an end of student acquisition of applied skills.

The author clearly remembers an IEP team meeting when the parents reported an important family outcome that their child could not drink from a glass without spilling liquid all over his clothes and table. The family enjoyed occasionally going out to eat, and when the child spilled his drink, other people in the restaurant would stare at the parents and other siblings, making everyone in the family feel uneasy and conspicuous and causing the family to not enjoy going out to eat together. The child was of the size, to an unsuspecting public, that he should be able to drink without making a mess. This was a very important outcome to the family. Surprisingly this was not known or reported by the school, even though the student ate lunch at school.

As this information was shared with the IEP team, the occupational therapist and the speech pathologist immediately said they could work on lip closure, upper extremity coordination, and swallowing skills. The special education teacher could work with the lunchroom staff and offered assistance during the resource period. This became a goal on the IEP, and parents learned from school personnel how to assist in the teaching of drinking skills.

The student quickly learned to drink appropriately, and the family started to again enjoy opportunities to go out to eat as a family without feeling that others were paying attention to them. The quality of the experience and the application of skills in natural environments made a significant difference at school and at home, and in the community.

A simple outcome presented by the parents from observation and the parents' evaluation not only led to a functional goal on the IEP but provided a valuable and meaningful service to the student and his family.

This is how outcomes and discipline recommendations become collaborative goals. An IEP goal to reduce the frequency of disruptive behaviors to peers in class also applies at home and in the community. The approaches used at school are also carried out at home in as similar a fashion as possible. The goal to understand the main theme of a written paragraph is reinforced at home during a scheduled short reading time as it was during a Title 1 reading session.

The goal to increase math proficiency to a third grade level is supported on family grocery store trips and recreation events as it is during math time in an elementary school. These are collaborative goals and goals that improve the quality of the student's life.

These goals and coordination of services do not just happen; they are developed by a continuous IEP process of sharing information as equal partners in a team effort. All participants are respected, and information is treated as important data necessary to make educational decisions leading to success and achievement. Even when IEP team members may change each school year, the commitment to collaboration and equal participation will follow the student and the IEP team.

Collaboration and coordination may need some training for school personnel and for parents. The next chapter will discuss IEP team member training for outstanding IEPs.

ANALYSIS

1. How should IEP goals be determined?
2. Why is it important to understand the recommendations of all assessments, including the parents?
3. What can you do, as chair of the IEP team meeting, to construct meaningful goals from a variety of discipline evaluations and recommendations?

EVALUATION

1. What recommendations were discussed in the team meeting?
2. How did the team review recommendations and make decisions about each recommendation?

3. Were recommendations discussed in a collaborative framework for student achievement and success?
4. How did goals evolve in the discussion of the recommendations and participant input?
5. Did the goals decided by the team reflect current skill sets and skill needs in natural environments?
6. Do the goals reflect the hopes and dreams of the student, parents, and the school staff?

12

Team Member Training

KEY POINTS

1. It is very important to provide adequate parent training to introduce them to the IEP process.
2. School staff need training to understand the collaborative nature of the IEP team.
3. Develop a school and district culture of collaboration.

It may seem that parents need the most training for effective and outstanding IEP development, and this is probably true. However, school personnel who attend IEP team meetings (and most teachers) also require training. This is the leader's job to do! This effort is, again, a situation of "Pay now or pay later!"

Through training of parents and school personnel, the leader will be developing a norm, a practice for outstanding IEP team meetings, and a culture for your school and district. As the culture expands to all parents and school staff, the training efforts become easier and permeate all IEP processes: eligibility, placement, annual and three-year reviews, and IEP development.

Teaching parents to become equal partners starts in the development of a purposeful and welcoming culture to the IEP process. (See chapter 8.) Many parents understand the IEP team meeting to be a war zone.

This is communicated between parents having bad experiences and others who tell of their misfortunes to other parents. This is the norm that needs to change, and the change begins with a small group session with the IEP team leader and parents to explain the collaborative nature of the IEP process, what to expect, and what to say during the team meetings. Explain the parents' evaluation; the collection of observational data into the learned, emerging skills; the outcomes; and collaboration efforts between school and home. Help parents to know the basic laws (federal and state) and the mandates that are applied to the school.

The key, however, is to sincerely and overtly express the collaborative nature of the process, the interest the school staff has in understanding the student at home and in the community, and the willingness the school personnel have to work together to develop an education plan that is effective. This training is important not only to explain the collaborative nature of your district's IEP team meetings, but to start to dispel the negative perspective many parents have toward the process and meetings.

Of course it is easy to say nice things and use the right words during training and the IEP team meeting; now the IEP leader and school staff will need to prove it by doing what is said is going to happen. This means the leader must teach the school personnel the same things, the laws and mandates, the impact of evaluations, the welcoming, and sharing of information in a way that leads toward IEP goal development.

This may be a more difficult task than the parent training. School personnel are going to be pressed for time, do not understand the rationale of the IEP process, and see little importance in creating more paperwork for themselves. However, the leader will need to keep in mind that the very same concern exists for the parents.

Creating a school culture is difficult, and resources are necessary; mostly time.

Remember the pay now or later paradigm! With an intention of creating outstanding IEPs, take the time to plan effective training for parents and teachers, do some training together, and involve the school administration and school board members. The leader will need to demonstrate commitment and the district's interest in making great IEPs a school norm.

Leaders' efforts and the time of parents and teachers will save tons of hours later on. Just like teaching a sequential skill to students, the easy parts are taught first so that the harder steps become less difficult later on. The same is true for the teaching of parent and teacher skills for IEP development. You will need to create a culture of welcoming, equal partnerships, and meaningful experiences within the IEP system.

STUDENT TRAINING

Many districts provide educational venues to help students learn how to advocate for themselves within a larger community context. For students with intellectual disabilities, autism, and vision and hearing impairments, learning how to express to others individual issues affecting their lives is an important educational service. Within the context of such training, it becomes an easy venue to teach students how to participate in the IEP team meetings.

This is not just done as a lecture or a presentation of what the IEP team meeting is about, who will be there, and what the team meeting will produce. Successful student training involves setting up mock IEP meetings offering practice with real teachers and specialists.

Students rehearse making statements of what is important to them, responding to information presented by others, and offering recommendations based upon student interests and future hopes. See appendix B.

Student training for IEP team meetings is not limited to just those students with intellectual and sensory disabilities, but to all special education students. This is a wonderful opportunity to teach appropriate meeting behaviors, self-control, relationship skills with adults, and advocating for oneself. This training goes far beyond the team meeting; skills for employment, social interactions, and teamwork are skills necessary as a successful adult.

A student is never too young to have this training, although the presentation and expectation need to be adjusted relationally to cognition and age. Even young students can participate by indicating their interests, saying what they would like to do as they get older, and even what they think they need to learn. Not only is it good practice for when students get a better understanding of adult aspirations, but the information is extremely useful to parents and school staff.

PARENT TRAINING

Parent training can be provided in small to medium-size groups at school with a few teachers and an administrator and perhaps a school board member. The training agenda should include very brief outlines of state mandates and federal law, a description of the collaborative IEP process, and a discussion of the parents' evaluation. *Hopes and Dreams: An IEP Guide for Parents of Children with Autism Spectrum Disorder* (Lentz, 2004), can serve as a great guide to work through the process of the collaborative IEP.

In this parent model, parents learn how to develop the parents' assessment using forms that they complete in the important areas: learned skills, emerging skills, student likes and interests, proposed educational outcomes, and recommendations for how the school and home can work together to teach, practice, and use emerging skill sets.

Input from school personnel is important for the parents to support the initiative and enhance the understanding of the IEP process. Ninety minutes

should be adequate with time for questions and informal after-meeting refreshments.

TEACHER TRAINING

Teachers should follow just about the same procedure, but reinforcing the
ground rules is important (chapter 8). Once it is stated what the espoused culture is, school staff will need to ensure it is the way it was said it was going
to be. Therefore teachers need to know exactly what was said to the parents.
This is the reason to have some teachers, administrators, and school board
members attend the parent training. Teachers and specialists should learn
how to explain testing procedures in a manner in which parents can understand why a specific testing protocol was used, how results were interpreted,
and why recommendations were derived from the testing procedures.

When a special education teacher reports, he or she should be able to explain the testing procedures: "I used the Brigance because this test had a better potential of assessing Jill's real academic skill levels. Some academic tests
compare scores to other students. This test only looks at Jill's skills now and
compares present skills to scores she demonstrated last year. Now we have a
comparison of one year's progress for Jill. This test was completed in several
time blocks and on a one-on-one basis, so stress from the test was minimal."

Evaluative information is used for all educational decision making by the
IEP team. Parents as well as school staff need a concise but formidable understanding of various discipline assessments and why specific testing protocols
were used.

Teachers and specialists need to learn and practice talking to the student—
the student is the main focus of the team meeting. Far too often, teachers and
specialists talk around the student. It is very beneficial for the school staff
to involve the student in the discussion of progress and assessment results.
Engage the student as much as possible.

School staff also needs to remember and to know how to make meaningful
and honest "good comments" about the parents' child, and your student. One
rule needs to be conveyed to all, one realistic and nice thing to say—every
student has something of value, and the culture you are attempting to create
mandates that every student has worth!

A true and well-meaning statement such as, "Jill listens very well to directions," or "John and his classmates are reading *Tom Sawyer* and he enjoys
the story and reads well, but I would like to see John be able to predict future
events in the story." I do remember a teacher saying, "I can't find anything
positive to say about this kid!" Another teacher responded, "Just say, 'good

blinking.'" Fortunately, another teacher looked over the progress the student had made and was thrilled to report that expressive language skills had improved over time!

While it is often very difficult, teachers and specialists need to be able to report and talk without the plethora of educational jargon, especially special education acronyms and esoteric terms. I used to cringe many times as I heard, "Splintered skills really interfered with any norm-reference testing procedures, especially for kids like John with ASD, because CA and MA scores produced a skewed IQ, especially verbal scores. However, I believe ESY will be a good idea, and SI should be introduced in the IEP; however I don't see much different from last year's PLOP (present level of academic performance)." Oh, my!

Parent and teacher trainings should be scheduled so each can attend one time a year, but realize that several trainings will need to be scheduled each year so all parents and teachers can attend in small and intimate groups. This training can happen during the summer or near the start of the school year, and it can be very powerful to have experienced parents and teachers present parts of the training.

As efforts move forward, trained parents and teachers would not need to attend each year. However, for parents, and teachers too, training should be expected as children move to different school buildings—between elementary to middle and middle school to high school.

ANALYSIS

1. How can your district enhance training for parents and school staff to create a culture of collaboration for the IEP process?
2. Why is it important to train school staff to participate in IEP meetings?
3. What will you do to take parent and school staff training for collaborative IEPs to the next level?

EVALUATION

1. Did student training occur?
2. Did student training include a practice IEP with other persons "attending"?
3. Did you feel the student training was productive and meaningful for the student?
4. Did parent training occur?

5. Did parents have an opportunity to learn about the parents' assessment and complete forms that included learned and emerging skills, parent outcomes, and how to coordinate outcomes with the school?
6. Did some teachers, school staff, and administrators or school board members attend?
7. Did you feel parent training was productive and meaningful for parents?
8. Did teacher training occur?
9. Did teachers have an opportunity to learn and practice reporting in a clear and concise manner and watch the use of acronyms?
10. Did teachers gain an understanding of the collaborative nature of the team meeting?

13

Follow-Up

The Paperwork

KEY POINTS

1. All of the good intentions of an outstanding IEP are void if the paperwork is late and the written IEP misrepresents the concepts developed at the team meeting.
2. Paperwork and all documents must be completed and distributed in a timely fashion and within federal and state timelines.
3. Follow-up to any IEP team meeting involves paperwork!

Once the IEP team meeting is concluded, all required paperwork needs to be completed and done in a timely fashion. If the IEP team meeting was a third-year reevaluation or an annual IEP review, the IEP will need to be written or modified to reflect the decisions made during the team meeting. If the team meeting was to determine eligibility or placement, required paper likewise needs to be completed in a timely and precise fashion. It will be essential that the writing of the IEP or modifications accurately state the outcomes of the team members.

The value of the IEP is twofold. First it sets the educational plan for the student, and second, it confirms the collaborative nature of the IEP team meeting. The first point is obvious, as all of the components of the IEP spell out what will actually happen outside of methodology that is not part of the IEP. However, methodologies should be shared with the parents so parents can support IEP goals at home and in the community.

The second point is equally important because if it accurately reflects what was discussed and agreed upon during the team meeting, then parents and teachers will have a real sense that the culture of the district is not only

113

espoused, but it is what really happens. This level of confidence will go far into the student's life during his or her entire school experience.

Follow-up is important. The development and the writing of the IEP may seem to be the end of the process; however, it actually is the beginning. From the point of the IEP being written and distributed to all appropriate persons, the district then has a legal responsibility to activate the conditions of the IEP exactly as written, or as agreed upon.

The IEP contains not only goals and in some cases short-term objectives but also related services, modifications, and accommodations that need to be implemented as stated on the IEP. Implementation must occur in all areas of the student's daily school life, so every teacher and related service staff person must be aware of the IEP and know to what extent each area and classroom needs to follow through on IEP responsibilities.

Implementation of the IEP and the construction of the IEP are the major reasons for most of the mediations, due process hearings, and civil actions between parents and schools. Hundreds of school administration hours and many dollars from constricted education financial resources are required from school districts for mediators and courts to decide or remediate parent complaints.

Even though there are many students with IEPs, follow-up must occur to ensure that all facets of the IEP are being serviced to the student in the manner in which such services were intended to be implemented. This fits into the culture of outstanding IEPs and, of course, the delivery of specific IEP services. You really do "pay now or pay a whole lot later."

ANALYSIS

1. How does follow-up to team meetings reflect a "pay now or pay later" philosophy?
2. Why is written documentation a statement of your school or district's culture?
3. What are you going to do to ensure that paperwork is part of the school norm?

EVALUATION

1. Did all paperwork get completed within ten school days from the date of the team meeting?
2. Did all participants of the team meeting receive a copy of the reports or IEP or modifications and revisions to the IEP?

3. Did the paperwork accurately reflect the intentions and discussions that occurred during the team meeting?
4. Are recommendations, goals, and supports agreed upon at the team meeting implemented during school time?
5. Are recommendations, goals, and supports agreed upon at the team meeting implemented at home and in the community?
6. Is the culture at the school and in the district supportive toward collaboration with the school staff, parents, and students?

Part II Summary

The IEP process can be a wonderful experience for educators and parents. Great things can happen for students and parents and teachers when school and home work toward the same outcomes, share mutual respect, and work in a collaborative manner. It can be very satisfying to be part of a real team focused upon and striving toward student achievement.

Too often the IEP team meeting gets a negative rap from parents and school staff. This is too bad; the IEP is the most important aspect of the student's school life, and the IEP team concept is just waiting for this to be a collaborative arrangement with potential just around the corner.

Outstanding IEPs require a great team. Great teams are built, and don't just happen to fall into place. To build great teams, school personnel need to be mindful of the following:

1. Present accurate and factual information and base recommendations upon these data and multiple observational data, not just one-time observations.
2. Justify recommendations with a statement of why the recommendations or observations are important.
3. Provide good and respectful training and interactions with parents.
4. Do not justify reasons for putting or not putting something in the IEP because of state and federal laws and mandates—this does not hold water for parents or students. It will minimize the school staff reputation and ability to conduct outstanding IEPs by projecting that the intent of the meeting and the IEP is to comply with rules, not student interests.
5. Keep reporting to the point; individual reports should never last for more than five minutes. Be prepared and concise. Others can ask questions if necessary. Keep all reporting relevant to the student.

6. Do what is right for the student. If there is a question of applicability to current laws, work for what is right for the student, and then massage what is right into something that loosely can be tied into the regulations; not the other way around. If it is good for the student, it fits the spirit of the law even when the letter of the law may be slightly compromised.

    It is easier to explain why this is done if the actions were for student achievement rather than try to rule by law over the individual needs of the student. At one IEP annual review, the team (including the parents and student) felt that improving the student's social skills was immensely important, but the district had a policy that all IEP goals must be directly aligned with the state standards for educational delivery. With some ingenuity the director of special education wrote that the student will increase appropriate social and citizenship skills by 25 percent as a social studies–aligned goal. The spirit was clearly stated, the letter to the law, and it worked well! Actually the student improved social skills with peers and school staff on his way to becoming a better citizen as an adult. This was "right" for the student.

7. Let parents know that the school's staff appreciates what parents do on an everyday basis and thank the parents for their participation, even if they become confrontational or do not actively participate. They were there!

8. Help draw information pertinent to a discussion by asking for parent input; what have you seen when . . ., how do you deal with . . ., what do think about. . . . Do this during all team meetings and with all team members. Ask parents and teachers if such statements reflect what they have seen in classrooms and at home.

9. Do not be afraid of using short-term objectives (STO) even though they only apply to students using alternative assessments. There is no reason you cannot use STOs. This could be very important when a goal is complicated or rigorous.

    A series of STOs can help the student break down the goal into manageable steps and make accomplishments without having to complete the mastery level of such goals. The laws do not say STOs cannot be used, so if it fits, do what's right for the student.

10. Participate in the IEP team meeting like it is the most important thing a school staff has done the entire year—it is for the student and the parent. The manner of participation, excitement, and celebration of achievement and progress will carry on the future IEPs and student success. Be part of the party!

Outstanding IEPs happen for a reason; people care and people produce. Every effort needs to be made at the beginning of the process; getting parents and teachers off to the right start will go miles in our attempts to develop and construct meaningful and purposeful educational plans for children with disabilities.

Start with the training and then do what you say you are going to do—district-wide! If this happens, you will enjoy years of interesting and valuable discussions of the best options for students to find success that will continue for the rest of the students' lives.

TRANSFORMATION OF THE IEP TEAM

INTRODUCTION

This third section is a description of how the IEP team can make significant changes in school efficiency and effectiveness. This is now possible because of the changes that occurred when transformational leadership guided the IEP team. In very simple terms, transformational leadership causes organizational transformation.

Transformational leadership has been discussed within a theoretical framework described in part I and by the application process presented in part II. This third part will discuss several important topics related to organizational transformation that are directly influenced by the characteristics of a learning organization, transformational leadership, and the use of these principles to improve IEP team meetings and IEPs.

It is clear that quality improvement efforts in schools and public accountability for educational effectiveness are in demand by government officials as well as the general public. For years into the future there will most likely be government and public demands for superior performance and greater degrees of efficiency requirements.

The way educators demonstrate effectiveness today will probably never get close to meeting the future expectations and legislative standards. Even while great things are happening in our schools across the country, the public demands for taxpayer satisfaction will only increase as the public realizes that education is a high-price state expenditure.

The burden of accountability will also be increased for special education services. For a school district to demonstrate effectiveness in special education, the district will need to demonstrate success beyond the state-required test scores and standardized testing (this is also true for the "regular kids" in schools, but this is a larger discussion). Accountability is an increasing concern in special education as well as the entire K–12, and actually K–16, educational system.

Part III will explore four central themes to demonstrate program effectiveness and to guide initiatives for a continuous quality improvement program. The author believes that the application of the following four topical areas should be attempted after persons and IEP teams have been introduced to the learning organization and transformational leadership attributes of the IEP team found in part I and the application of the manner of improving the leading of the IEP team discussed in part II.

With this knowledge base and the experience of reaching out to other school staff, students with disabilities, parents, and the community, the transformational leader has the ability and opportunity to make a larger transformation; that of the school.

The transformation of the school is a slow process, but it can start with a simple IEP team that disregards the status quo. This happens when the IEP team is willing go outside of the team's comfort zone and begins a venture into the drive to improve team functions and student services. There is really nothing very new here, just ideas that can be carried out by a transformational leader and team to impact the success and achievement of students in the school with disabilities and those without.

The section will start in chapter 14 by asking the readers to think of the IEP as more than one single event or just one written plan. Teams need to consider the IEP as a series of IEP team meetings over time; one IEP evolves into another. Then chapter 15 will move into a discussion that integration is more than just a classroom with a few students with disabilities sitting in; integration goes far beyond the classroom. Chapter 16 will discuss the need to eliminate the educational system of the negatives that often drive either educational reform or educational implementations. The last chapter will provide a brief look at transforming the special education process to shed some light on what may happen in the future, and at least stir up some emotions about what we should be concerned about or connected to today.

The author hopes this part III will cause some discomfort with the way we do things now, while starting a plan for the future. The course to be taken is left for the reader and the transformational leader. However, it is hoped that more questions are raised than answered, that the unsettling issues that may be stirred up will project a movement to quality improvement, and discussion of IEP improvement will really make a difference for students in our schools with disabilities. This is up to the reader.

14

Think of the IEP Team Meeting as a Series of Successes

KEY POINTS

1. Teams that treat the IEP as a single event miss opportunities to meet student needs.
2. IEPs that are considered as a series of planning meetings develop comprehensive and future-planning initiatives.
3. Problems under a sequencing IEP process are identified and dealt with effectively, rather than with one-time fixes seen in single-event-type IEP team meetings.

Far too often leaders or chairs of IEP team meetings think only about the event of the team meeting as both a one-time occurrence and something that just needs to get done. The discussion throughout this writing has been toward not thinking about the IEP as a single event or as a chore. The discussion has been one that has viewed the IEP team and an IEP as a series of meetings that will shape the education services received by a student with disabilities through a coordinated plan of educational services over time.

The reason such emphasis has been and is placed on the concept that an IEP team meeting is not a single event is that there will always be another IEP team meeting, there is always another decision that the team will need to make, and there are always updates and communications circulating between IEP team members. The IEP team does not stop until the student graduates, leaves the K–12 system, or fails to qualify for continued special education services.

Troubles begin early when a chair or leader considers the IEP team meeting as a single event. The main trouble with a single-IEP paradigm is that the idea of planning for future IEPs goes away. Long-term planning is the length of time guessed by the team necessary for student goals to be learned or mastered. Therefore, in a single-event paradigm, long-term planning is about one year.

When single-event meetings occur, there are few efforts made to build upon relationships between the student and the parents and little planning to think beyond the immediate goals and skill deficits, especially as the IEP team deals with transition planning.

Most teams working under the single-event leadership style have difficulty considering next steps in sequential goals, in transition planning, and going beyond the classroom environment. These issues severely impact the effectiveness of the IEP and the special education service delivery process. Such teams considerably and negatively impact student learning and functional skill achievement. This may be a good time to go back and review the Git-er done types introduced in chapter 1.

Different attitudes about the IEP take place when IEP teams think of an IEP as a part of a student's life. The idea is that the IEP meeting is only part of a series of IEP meetings about the specific student for all school years, K–12. What is discussed at one meeting will be examined during the next meeting. Ideas shared during an IEP team meeting may become goals or supports at the present IEP meeting and at another meeting in the future.

The degrees of interactions increase or decrease between parents, students, and school staff as IEP team members continue meeting currently and into the future. The level of cooperation and feelings toward collaboration carry over from one meeting to another. All of these issues portray a different response when one thinks of an IEP series rather than a single event.

The IEP as a series also projects itself to a theory-in-use that is easily observable to all team members. When the leader, usually a transformational leader, treats the IEP team meeting like it is a sequence of progressive meetings, team members can see the difference in the manner by which the meeting is chaired. This difference can be also evident throughout the school and district as students with disabilities are making progress and by the coordination of services and school staff.

In the single-event meeting, ideas probably will be dismissed easily with no records kept of what was discussed, goals that were suggested will not be documented, and transition planning will be very short-sighted and without sufficient detail to be effective to ascertain plans leading to student success as an adult.

Recommendations in a single-event paradigm for further evaluation or assessment will be pushed aside, and supplemental aids and supports will be sketchy and almost inoperable due to the operational vagueness and lack of program description. These single-event IEP team meetings are not necessarily rare; they may be prevalent and occur in nearly every school district.

The IEP as a series looks very different. The meeting is constructed in a way that all information, ideas, and suggestions are recorded. The future as well as the present is discussed, and steps are taken to ensure that functional skill acquisitions are broken down to realistic goals. The outcomes of students and parents are always deemed important and are maintained for use in current as well as successive meetings.

Often a transformational leader will say things such as, "Let's keep this in mind for the next meeting," or "John, what do you think about a job at the convenience store perhaps next year when you are sixteen?" The discussion is much more than what is required to be done during an IEP team meeting; it is really about the future of the student with disabilities.

Considering IEP team meetings as a series also builds relationships and develops teamwork. In chapter 3 it was discussed that relationships are built over time and start with teams doing what teams say they do. This was reinforced in chapter 10 when the team planned for collaborative educational outcomes.

If the school has embraced the learning organization and transformational leadership principles from part I, and if the team is led by following the steps in part II, the application of sequencing IEPs should fall right into place. The basis for relationship development and enhancement is established. The IEP, when treated as a series of planning initiatives, treats the persons on the team differently also. The persons on the team are treated as experts, as partners in a process, and as leaders to evoke change.

The attitudes of thinking about the IEP as a sequence by the IEP team members can have a direct positive impact on the remediation or treatment of IEP dissatisfaction from parents or school staff. When dissatisfaction occurs in a single-event type of IEP arrangement, the typical remedy for the single event is another single event like mediation, a hearing, or other type of one-time remediation attempt. This result of mediation or a hearing is a one-time fix.

The one-time fix is only that—it fixes whatever disagreement or dissatisfaction only one time. There are no efforts to present a long-term problem-solving measure, or even a route for disagreeing parties to follow at the next IEP team meeting. It's a one-time remedy. The problematic issue is rarely solved as a long-term solution. The outcome is a one-time fix of the symptoms of core issues, and the problem does not really go away; it festers and will probably reach a more heightened degree of dissatisfaction the next time the team meets.

When the IEP is operated as a series of collaborative meetings, any relationship problems or disagreements are typically addressed by the team as part of the ongoing discussion. This occurs because (a) the team members are prepared to discuss outcomes and the current status of the student, (b) the student is actively engaged in the process, and (c) the team has built a manner for consensus and honest relationships. The collaborative team knows that problems or disagreements are solved at the root issue by the team in a team meeting before other topics can be discussed.

Team members understanding the IEP as a series know that there are no effective one-time fixes, that any issues perceived by any team member must be resolved so the team can resume its collaborative duties now and for all future meetings. Problems are solved as part of the existing culture and norms of the IEP team.

Students learn skills as a series of learning activities. A student learns addition and subtraction before the student learns how to balance and maintain a checkbook, and a student learns to read at a certain grade level before more difficult reading comprehension is expected. This is scope and sequence of the curriculum. The same must be thought of when thinking about the IEP team.

Goals are almost always progressive; they lead to a higher degree of learning or a higher criterion for mastery. Goals should move the student toward purposeful outcomes, real skills that are used at home, in school, and within community environments. Likewise, the IEP team must align to the same paradigm; IEPs are progressive over time. The team needs to always be thinking about the "next steps," the future, and the transition plan concept.

Transition planning needs to start at the first IEP, even if the student is eight years old. This is necessary because the entire nature of transition is movement toward independence as a successful adult. What is typically thought when educators hear the words *transition planning* is a prescribed meeting plan to address adult needs.

True, but transition must successfully occur with movement from an elementary to a middle school, a middle to high school, as well as successful transitions from the K–12 system to adulthood. Even transition from year to year to new classrooms and teachers may need to be considered.

Transitions in all forms, such as moving from one classroom to another, changing schools, and leaving the K–12 system, are difficult for many students with disabilities. Planning for any transition, even from one activity to another, must be a designed effort.

Formal transition planning also needs to start well before the age specified by the special education law. The actual and common thoughts about transition are often too difficult and entrenched for a school person to do all that is required by the law to be accomplished. This needs to be a team activity with heavy parent and student input and involvement. This is an important reason to engage parents AND STUDENTS in the IEP process in the earliest of stages.

The premise is that the IEP is a series of sequential meetings designed to meet the changing and developing needs of the student. When the team accepts the sequencing nature of the IEP, the team is then able to prepare a series of IEP team meetings with future planning, to express the outcomes for the goals and supports included in one IEP with a plan for the outcome of that goal as a learned acquisition for the student. Likewise the sequencing prepares the team to deal effectively with transitions and to enhance collaborative and meaningful team relationships.

ANALYSIS

1. How does the concept of an IEP as a series affect the perception of IEP teams in schools?
2. Why do remediation efforts focus on a one-time fix of a symptom of a problem, not a long-lasting remedy or a way of dealing with the core problem?
3. What can you do to promote a sequencing concept of IEP team meetings?

EVALUATION

1. Do team members of IEP teams at your school consider team meetings as singular events or as a series of meetings to develop progressive IEPs over time?
2. What can you do as a transformational leader to support and reinforce the IEP series concept?
3. Are disagreements and dissatisfaction issues treated as a one-time fix or within the context of the team meeting as a long-term solution?
4. What is your role to help attitudes of solution-finding initiatives?
5. How does the team function as a relationship-building experience in your school?
6. What can you do to reinforce the need to project a future-planning philosophy with the IEP team members?
7. What is the perception of the IEP toward transition planning?

15

Integrate More Than Just the Classroom

KEY POINTS

1. Integration and inclusion are practices that need to be implemented in full—NOW.
2. The IEP is a change agent to expedited inclusion and to assist in effectiveness.
3. Teacher licenses must be integrated as a co-teacher license.
4. The curriculum needs to be integrated for all students.
5. Related services are necessary, but scheduling is very important.

Educators have been discussing integration of students with disabilities into regular education for the past two decades. What was originally thought of as mainstreaming, then integration, is now considered inclusion with a response to intervention (RTI) and differentiated learning (DL) as a practice to improve student success in the inclusion classroom and school. There are hundreds of references and research studies demonstrating that inclusion works for students with disabilities AND students without disabilities.

Most educational experts advocate including children in regular classrooms with appropriate levels and types of supports. Therefore, many schools are committed to reducing and eliminating resource rooms, special education self-contained rooms, and the exclusion of students with disabilities from any form of many school activities.

The RTI and DL models have provided a significant pathway for special education inclusion. RTI has made data-based decision making, collaboration, and a multilevel paradigm of supports available to all students, not just those students receiving special education.

This model has reduced the "specialness" of special education because supports become individualized and assessment of student achievement is based on more than scores and rankings. As RTI becomes universally used, the model will support inclusion of all students and supports not an obtuse departure from what many other students receive in a school.

Similarly DL provides a pathway for inclusion because DL requires a variety of teaching methodologies, assignments, and assessments to individually include all students. As seen by RTI, DL removes some of the specialness of service delivery previously seen only in special education, for special education students. While DL was designed for diverse learners, the concepts are appropriate for all students.

As teachers, administrators, and resource professionals learn and apply facets of DL and RTI in schools and classrooms, the impact on those students receiving special education and district efforts to support fully integrated classrooms will find greater success due to the individualization and variety of methodologies, instruction, and assessments afforded to all students.

After all these years, the amount of research, and practices supporting inclusion, RTI, and DL, educators and education systems just need to stop restricting opportunities for students with disabilities from typical school opportunities. It just needs to stop.

All children should be able to attend classes, activities, cocurricular, and any other school event without being classified as special, exceptional, or disabled. The time is now that all students are fully included with all students of the school.

Research and best practices have been available to teachers, schools, and administrators for a long time. It should not be a surprise or even be news that a certain school district or a specific school is implementing a totally inclusive school environment for students with disabilities. This today should not be newsworthy; this should be a theory-in-use, a common and expected practice.

The degree of research and existing practices, the how-to procedures are there; they need a transformational leader to start the change at the local education level and with the individual IEP team to provide programmatic direction through an individual IEP.

The practice of a totally inclusive school actually can start with the manner in which an IEP is developed and constructed. Each IEP must indicate how and how often the student will be engaged with nondisabled peers in inclusive classrooms. This is where the culture of a school and district comes into play—the culture needs to explicitly state that all students deserve to receive their education in a classroom and with their peers, with just enough individual supports to provide student success.

There is a tendency for many schools to espouse a view that students receive "inclusive educational opportunities" but only in physical education, art, music, and perhaps other non-core-content areas. All students need to receive all their education in all content areas in an integrated classroom supporting differentiated learning opportunities. Realistic and effective supports must be provided to assist the student in nondiscriminatory and overly exemplified ways.

The supports cannot be the elephant in the room; supports need to be discreet, effective, and normalizing. Supports developed by the IEP team with the guidance of a transformational leader can construct the IEP to be implemented throughout a school and the school day without drawing abnormal attention either to the supports or the student.

It will be the manner in which the IEP is written that will offer an increased measure of student success. Goals and supports must be adaptable for integrated classrooms, not stated to be implemented only in a resource room or a self-contained classroom. It is easy to write goals to be presented only in self-contained and resource rooms, and it will take some effort to construct the individual student goals to be applicable throughout the school environment.

INTEGRATION OF TEACHERS

With the total inclusion of all students in a school or district, there is a rationale for an integrated or co-teacher license. This is a license that is a combination of a content-area major and emphasis of equivalent course work for a special education certification or degree. At most teaching colleges, content-area student teachers must take a three-credit course on disabilities or exceptional education and a course on diversity and education of a diverse classroom. That is it.

It is unfathomable to consider what could be done with a math teacher with enough special education background and postemployment training to apply social skills training (Dunn, 2006), or a five-point scale (Dunn-Buron, 2003) for a student with Asperger's taking an advanced math class. Or imagine a middle school teacher using discrete trial to work on a science lesson, or even an elementary teacher using a strategy to help a student with learning disabilities to find the key sentence or topic of a written paragraph.

Special education teachers would continue to be employed but would serve as a resource and to prescribe certain difficult methodologies for students needing significant supports. However, all students would be educated in the "regular" classroom with their nondisabled peers.

An integrated and comprehensive co-teacher license would provide an academic background in a core content area and knowledge of special education methodology and strategies with a cross-categorical special education license. This cross-categorical license includes subject material covering all of the IDEA disability categories and specific educational and behavioral strategies that have been considered as effective teaching methodologies.

The author is not necessarily a fan of the cross-categorical license for special education. It would better serve students for the special education teacher to have a specific license for the disabilities categorized under IDEA such as learning disabilities or intellectual disability special education teachers. The cross-categorical license would be accepted as a co-teacher or integrated license, with a license in specific grades or content area.

INTEGRATED CURRICULUM

Integrating the curriculum means that states and local education agencies develop and maintain a rigorous set of content-area standards, or even a rich national education curriculum in each content area. All students would be required to demonstrate the ability to be knowledgeable and to apply skill sets included in state or national performance standards.

The role of the IEP team would allow a certain degree of flexibility in how the standard applies to students eligible for special education services. The team, again under the guidance of a transformational leader, would discuss and suggest ways for the spirit of the standard to be adapted to fit the short- and long-term needs of the student with disabilities.

An integrated curriculum must be more flexible than most state and local curricula are presently. Especially when an IEP team is working with a student with cognitive and learning disabilities, the extent or the degree to which a curricular standard is known by the student needs to be weighed against its use by the student in a natural environment or event.

Like the curriculum seen across the country, curriculum is built around state standards, so it also is an integrated curriculum. As just stated, there needs to be flexibility in standards if standards are going to have meaning and function in a student's life. This is not a statement for only those students receiving special education; this statement is very true for all students.

State standards apply to the 68 percent of students who fall into the "normal academic or intelligence" population of U.S. students. For this majority of students, standards indicate the skills average students need to have knowledge of and hopefully apply throughout their lives. Standards do not apply in the same way for the 16 percent on either end of this bell curve. It would be grossly unfair and derelict if a district or state were to accept the same level of knowledge of a standard from the average and the gifted student.

Similarly for those students in the second and lower standard deviation below mean, they need to have a standard, but as with the gifted student, the degree of understanding and application needs to be flexible. Standards need to be a guide to what is taught at different grade levels, not an unbending and inflexible mandate for all students.

Standards could be considered like speed limits on interstate highways. A speed limit is a law of maximum and often minimum speeds. Drivers can get a fine if traveling outside the posted speed limits. Most drivers drive the average speed; however, not all. Every driver and passenger has seen police cars exceed the posted speed limit. Persons usually understand this and say, "It's okay for a policeman to go faster than the posted speed limit; there must be an accident ahead." Likewise travelers have seen trucks and cars pulling very heavy and big loads going slower than the minimum speed. In the same fashion, travelers say, "It's okay for that heavy load to be going slower, because the truck will need a lot more time to slow down in an emergency than the time required from a passenger car."

State standards need the same level of understanding if students with disabilities and students with many talents are going to succeed in school. Standard skills must apply to function and to application.

In chapter 2 the Test of Utility was introduced, and this should be reviewed as it applies directly to an integrated curriculum. Skills and standards may need to be adapted to best fit with an individual student, but that is the purpose of an individual education plan!

INTEGRATED RELATED SERVICES

Related services are those special services and interventions that provide for certain and specific student needs. For example, related services may include speech and language therapy, physical and occupational therapy, counseling, psychological, social work, and nursing. These services are directed by the IEP team and are written into the student's IEP. Many times the services provided by related service personnel to the student are scheduled at the convenience of the staff specialist, and many times the students are taken away to receive related services during important classroom instruction.

Efforts toward carving out time for the student to receive these important skills yet not jeopardize instruction in content areas need to be carefully considered. There may be ways for related services to be part of the instructional activity in the integrated classroom. For example, physical therapy could occur during physical education or recess in the elementary school, or counseling during the time in which a student may have the most difficulty in a school day, such as time after the student eats lunch or during a study hall in high school.

Obviously this will not work for everyone, and there will be times that the provision of a related service will not be held at the best time for the student. Likewise the complexity of the applied strategy or nature of the recommended related service may need to occur during important instructional time.

The team will need to accommodate the overall needs of the student as best as very possible; the accommodations must be driven by student needs, not vacant scheduling holes in the related service staff's calendar. However, the concept is to coordinate and integrate the related services so the student is not missing out with peers or instructional time.

ANALYSIS

1. How is the IEP a vehicle to initiate and improve an inclusionary school for all students?
2. Why is a co-teacher license important for the effectiveness of an integrated school?
3. What can you do to use the IEP team to greatly enhance the appreciation of inclusion for all students in your school or district, and how can you inspire a deeper and richer attitude of inclusion for diverse learners through the IEP process?

EVALUATION

1. How can you measure the degree to which integration occurs at your school?
2. What can you do to inspire other teachers to appreciate inclusion for all students?
3. Whom do you need to consider as key change agents to improve the inclusionary efforts of your school?
4. What are the prevailing attitudes in your school about students with disabilities not being in a self-contained classroom or a resource room during some or most of the day?

5. What is the availability of current research and best practices demonstrating the success of inclusion and integration in other schools and districts?
6. What are your ideas of a co-teacher license?
7. Where do you believe difficulty of an integrated curriculum will persist in your school or the IEP teams you serve on?

16

Eliminate the Negatives

Consequences Don't Rule

KEY POINTS

1. Negative threats and consequences affect all issues surrounding special education.
2. Great IEP teams and great IEPs are a good defense against negative perceptions held by the public about special education.
3. Accountability presents a great threat in special education now, as before accountability was not a primary threat to special education.
4. Use of community resources and persons has a positive effect on the perception of special education and students receiving special education services.

Negative thoughts and perceptions surround the entire arena of education. Perhaps recently such thoughts are more pronounced than previously, but negative perceptions of education and special education persist and cause problems in the delivery of education services. In special education, great IEPs can potentially reverse negative characteristics and perceptions within a district. Great IEPs can improve delivery of services in response to negative criticism.

Much of this discussion, in previous chapters, has been around the premise of improving the IEP team and the IEP to create a positive school culture and IEP team leadership. Now it seems appropriate to look at the IEP as a means to eliminate the negative attributes that may exist in and with the IEP team, school, or the district.

Earlier it was discussed that in nearly every school there exists a fear of an IEP team or school doing something wrong in special education. There is always the threat of lawsuits and that legal consequences will come raining down on a district.

In some districts and with some administrators, the rule is, "Whatever the parents want for their special education child, the parents will get—that will keep us out of the courtroom!" In the process of transforming the IEP team and the IEP, negative consequences cannot rule or direct the manner in which services are provided.

Often a barometer of great schools providing great IEPs is the perception of the IEP team and school administration that their IEPs are coordinated and completed in collaboration with parents actively engaged in the IEP process. Also there is little that can be misinterpreted by school staff, students, and parents on the IEP. If IEP teams can relax about the interpretation of the IEP, consequences do not rule, and quality becomes the attribute to achieve.

In nearly every aspect at the local, state, and federal level there are just too many real and perceived negative mindsets in education. Issues relating to regular education, special education, costs, teacher quality, the federal department of education, state departments overseeing local instruction, children scoring badly on tests, late-night TV hosts with games suggesting that young people do not even know where their own state capital is, all run the gamut of let's reengineer education.

Unfortunately, the reengineering most persons seem to like is the education they personally received thirty, forty, sixty years ago. The negatives highlighted through the media, by education critics and politicians, posit that education is simply failing. Government cuts and the dwindling financial and staff resources exist everywhere, and yet educators are being required to teach more than ever in our county's history and with less money to do it. Negatives do rule education.

When negatives rule education, the negatives certainly dominate special education. For many years special education was off the spectrum of negative attitudes and perceptions, either because it seemed against the rules or norms to attack special education, or it was politically incorrect to do so. This safeguard is now gone; the public critique is the same for regular and special education.

Some of the negativity toward special education has been through the reporting requirements of No Child Left Behind. Annually schools must publish in a local newspaper the test score data from each district school at certain grade levels. Furthermore, the scores are disaggregated into six subgroups such as socially disadvantaged, disability, and various racial/ethnic subgroups.

As the minimum standards for advanced and proficient are rising toward the 100 percent required in 2014, more schools are falling into the dreaded classification as "a school in need of improvement." There is the possibility for "state-imposed sanctions" for repeating schools not evidencing enough advanced and proficient students in the core content areas.

As the local papers print out this data, the disaggregated data by subgroups is also being printed. The conclusion made by many citizens, taxpayers, is that it is students with disabilities that are "wrecking" our fine local schools by their poor test scores: "Our fine schools used to be good, like they were when I went to school."

As school finances are becoming increasingly tight, educators are now hearing from the public comments that were never heard much before. These comments were on topics that seemed to be void and off-limits of public opinion: ratios of teachers to special education students, equipment needed for certain students, number of related service personnel, four-year-old kindergarten, IEP paperwork, specialized private schools (even though they should all be integrated like public schools should be), one-on-one support, nursing care, home-based services, and time to teach these kids who "won't amount to much anyway!"

Negatives go beyond the lawsuits sometimes in special education or the dispute resolution method we use seemingly daily. Negatives come from our own communities and our own neighbors. Negatives severely affect education and can be disastrous for special education. This is why great IEP teams and great IEPs are so very important now.

Accountability in special education and evidence of learning are serious issues that need to be addressed. Test scores may not be the most accurate demonstration of progress, but something needs to be in place to show student learning in special education. The great IEP may be the answer.

Great IEPs will lead the student through the K–12 system toward adulthood. Assessing how well students do in their lives after K–12 may be the only means to assess effectiveness of the special education program and its related costs. Negatives will not threaten or rule when great IEPs are in place.

Great IEP teams work toward collaboration, and a collaboration that extends beyond the IEP team. Bringing commerce and business into the special education program, having regular contacts with institutions of higher learning, and bringing the community performing and visual arts together to discuss the outcomes of special education become necessary for great IEP teams.

Business leaders and community activists should be represented on committees to find local avenues to include students with disabilities in the community. The transformational leader will share information so others can share ideas to promote inclusion and integration in naturally occurring community events and daily living experiences.

Great IEP teams reduce public criticism and negativity. Great teams build education substance and organizational strength. Great IEP teams bring forth great IEPs, and the outcomes of great IEPs are rich and meaningful.

ANALYSIS

1. How do various measures of special education accountability in your school affect the delivery of special education services?
2. Why are negative values and statements so commanding to teaching staff, administrators, and the public?
3. What can you do to project positive and meaningful information to school staff and the community about delivery of special education services?

EVALUATION

1. What can be done to improve public perception of special education in your community?
2. How can you engage the media to highlight services in your school?
3. How do negative attitudes rule in your department or school?
4. How can you communicate to others that great IEP team meetings can have a positive effect on school perceptions?
5. Can you cite a case in which the IEP team did remarkable things that resulted in improved feelings and school attitudes?
6. What ideas do you have to project to the community measures of accountability for special education services?

17

Transform the Process

Improve School Effectiveness

KEY POINTS

1. The transformational leader is able to promote quality improvement with IEP teams, greatly advancing the success of students receiving special education services.
2. Great IEP teams demonstrate an attribute of quality that can transcend an entire school and district.
3. School effectiveness initiatives and school culture change are long-term commitments.

It may be hard to imagine that the work of a single IEP team that does improve the IEP for one student can have a pervasive and valuable impact across the entire school environment. But it does. It works because this one team starts to develop a learning organization framework, and even though the content of an IEP team meeting is related to only one student, the spirit that arises from the team meeting and process becomes a flagship for educational services.

This great IEP will be different from anything else done at the school. The IEP team will start to embrace organizational effectiveness and improvements through the engagement of an improved and obviously changed perception of special education services.

Thinking of change originating from one IEP team and affecting an entire school culture is obviously a long-term engagement. However, it does have a tendency to move forward exponentially. This is a similar practice and quality improvement initiative ubiquitously used in business and industry. Small changes occur for one event or in one plant or one operation, and change

begins to occur, providing small but significant positive quality improvements. A snowball effect almost always occurs once the change is noted and
observed; the change and ancillary changes are practiced and ingrained into
the organizational norm and culture.

So how does the snowball effect really work? And how can an IEP really
make a difference? To answer these two questions, the reader will need to
look at this logistically, not theoretically. Every school experiences many IEP
team meetings every school year. The leader of an IEP team will chair many
IEP teams. One transformational leader/team chair introducing the learning
organization and quality improvement schemes to the IEP team and the written IEP actually influences several other IEP teams and school staff as well
as students and parents.

The transformation occurs for others through a well-conceived and con-
vincingly appropriate IEP with functional and implementable goals and supports. The strength of a team constructing such an IEP carries the momentum
of greatness to more integrated teachers applying supports and instruction
to meet the needs of one particular student. The pattern continues as regular
education teachers see value when students with disabilities are naturally
included in the classroom atmosphere and climate. Change begins to happen;
slowly, but predictably.

As the snowball, or the transformation, slowly journeys through a school,
the framework of a learning organization begins to support the attributes of
the learning organization and operational change. The learning organization
does not just happen because of a good idea or because a few teachers are
seeing positive impacts of great IEPs. Likewise the learning organization
did not necessarily begin with the positional leader, the principal, director
of special services, or superintendent. Often the learning organization begins
with a team leader willing to propel organizational change. Change, however,
cannot be accomplished alone; the transformational leader must be able to
motivate others to participate and believe in the change process. Organizational change occurs for one of two reasons.

The first reason for change is that the organization, the IEP team, school,
or district, must change due to external factors. These factors can include new
state and federal educational mandates, new rules and regulations, funding/
revenue limitations, and procedures. Change that is forced will never become
or lead toward transformation of a learning organization, yet most educational organization change occurs due to these factors.

The second reason for change will lead toward a potential to develop the
learning organization, and that is planned change. Learning organization
theorists such as Senge, Schoen, and Argyris do not project from where
leadership for creating or initiating the learning organization comes. Theo-

rists, however, are unified in stating that leadership can occur anywhere in any organizational structure and that the learning organization and the leadership of it are not natural activities. Movement from theory to practice is difficult.

The process of change in a learning organization, by an IEP team for example, begins and is maintained by either an administrator or a nonpositional leader and because the need for improved or great IEPs is more powerful than the difficulties of a change. Transformational leaders see change as a planned effort to produce a different and enhanced IEP and team.

There are many and various practices and theories for organizational change. Armenakis, Harris, and Mossholder (2000) proposed that learning organization and planned change are effectively designed through a six-step process: organizational readiness, diagnosis, feedback, planning change, intervention, and evaluation.

Lewin (1958) wrote that planned change occurs when the leader is able to "unfreeze" old behaviors, introduce new behaviors, and then freeze the new behaviors into organizational practices. Many other theorists have addressed a concept of planned organizational change. Usually the pundits of planned change view change on a large organizational platform. But meaningful change often begins on a micro-organizational operation, like the IEP team.

While being respectful to the theorists of organization development and learning organizations, a snowball effect for systemic change begins small, on the IEP team level. Not only is such a change manageable, but it allows the organization to grow with the slowly developing change initiative. The change does not happen overnight; it creeps into theories-in-use and daily practices, often unknowingly. This type of small organizational change is really uncomplicated and consists of four basic steps coordinated by the transformational leader: develop the change concept, sell it to stakeholders, implement the concept, and assess-modify.

The transformational leader develops the idea to improve IEPs to become great IEPs and learns the steps found in part II of this book and the conceptual frameworks in part I. This leader develops a vivid picture of how this team will function, projects how it will operate, and understands the steps necessary to move the idea forward.

Next the transformational leader will begin to sell the idea to team members. This can be as simple as stating (written or orally) to all team members—including parents and students—that the next IEP will be organized differently. The transformational leader will outline how it will be different and explain the new responsibilities of all team members. The team leader will individually follow up with all team members to ascertain their level of understanding of the IEP team change, new responsibilities, and what concerns each might have. The leader is then able to "sell" the idea on an individual basis.

The changes are implemented at the subsequent IEP team meeting. All team members will know that the first attempt may not be as smooth as it should be, but that the effort was different. Members then will start to assess the process and evaluate, possibly with a SWOT analysis discussed in chapter 4. The leader with the rest of the team will start to improve the new and changed IEP team based upon the evaluation of its implementation.

The snowball effect comes into play as this one IEP team begins to be recognized as a "new and improved" product and process. Recognition starts with team members experiencing the change process. Recognition at the start of a planned change activity can be negative or positive, but the word will start circulating throughout the school and possibly with parents and students. Most of the time, the message is clearly supportive, and enthusiastic reporting to others occurs. The snowball begins to grow.

The snowball effect happens rather easily and quickly. There are many IEP teams in a school; therefore, the transformational leader serves several IEP teams, special education teachers attend many IEP team meetings, and staff such as core-content-area teachers and related-services staff also attend many IEP team meetings.

The effort made in one student's IEP team meeting has a great opportunity to be spread through to other students' IEP team meetings. Students and parents will not have the opportunity to attend a variety of IEP team meetings, but the author can verify that parents and students will welcome the ideas and process described in part II.

As schools and classrooms become more and more integrated, regular education teachers will inherently become involved in the changing IEP process, as these teachers will be attending more IEPs. While there may be some core area teachers unfamiliar with the IEP process, the perception of the meeting will have a long-lasting effect. As more IEPs follow the process explained in part II, the IEP teams begin to variously change process and school culture. It all began with one interested transformational leader and one IEP team; it potentially influences an entire school.

AN EXAMPLE OF A SYSTEM OF PLANNED CHANGE

Armenakis, Harris, and Mossholder (2000) proposed that meaningful planned change in a learning organization follow a six-step process: organizational readiness, organizational diagnosis, feedback, planning change, intervention, and evaluation. How this six-step process involves the IEP team is theoretically presented to demonstrate this generally accepted planned change procedure. While this procedure is geared toward large-scale change, it will be important to see the likenesses and differences as the snowball effect just described on a much smaller basis.

Readiness

Using the IEP team with a desire to change begins with readiness. Most efforts to change organizational culture fail due to ineffective efforts to create a stakeholder mindset for the benefits of changing the status quo and apply new "behaviors" or procedures to the IEP team. The transformational leader of the IEP team will need to generate a need to engage in organizational change of the IEP team and share the needs of change to team members.

Changing the eligibility of the IEP team meeting as discussed in chapter 9 creates readiness for change by the nature of the changes to the entire IEP team meeting; new behaviors can start to be demonstrated and observed by parents, students, and school staff. Readiness sets the stage for improvement.

Diagnosis

The transformational leader, with all team members, should engage in a diagnostic effort to determine the strengths and weaknesses of the current IEP team process and the proposed new system. The diagnosis is best completed with questions and discussion from active IEP team stakeholders.

Questions from stakeholders will help the leader frame the learning organization and the transformation of the IEP team. Questions should be presented to all members of the team in an attempt for the transformational leader and all team members to understand the nature of the need for and concerns of change as well as gain an insight to the potential benefits of learning organizations.

Questions posed from the leader or members could be, "What is the kind of a culture that this IEP team will strive for?"; "What is the real purpose that this team will be engaged in, differently than now?"; "What are the daily norms of this new team that are projected to others in our entire organization?"; "How can this team influence greatness?" These questions will start the team thinking about possibilities, and the leader can gain insight to the members' readiness and willingness to move ahead in the learning organization process.

Feedback

Feedback allows the transformational leader to share input gained from the diagnosis with the IEP team members, and with all stakeholders in the school or district. Feedback communicates intention and readiness (if such is the case). Feedback to the team is most important at this stage. The communication to the team will map out problem areas, symptoms for readiness and fear of change, and cultural preparedness of team members.

Feedback from the transformational leader conveys trust and respect first to the IEP team members and second to the stakeholders. Trust of team members and stakeholders has the potential to lead to cooperative energy and efforts in the subsystem and the organization. The concept of the learning organization supports the very nature of trust. Honest feedback to members develops trust and builds relationships between all members that are essential in the learning organization. It moves the relationship of leaders and members to a higher moral and trustworthy plane that will heighten transformation of the IEP team.

Planning Change

The process to initiate a planned change is determined by the transformational leader and with IEP team members after completing the readiness and diagnosis phases. Since the planned change affects the IEP team members, planned change is dependent upon the assessment of the members' capacity to engage in the planned change. This assessment will determine the extent and the degree of change that the leader feels can be handled by the individual IEP team.

To plan for transformative change, the transformational leader must determine whether members will assist with or impede the proposed planned change. The leader should have a clear idea which stakeholders or members understand the process of the planned change, the degree to which members support the planned change, and whether or not the majority of members can actually start to move the IEP toward a learning organization.

The change parameters for this IEP team change begin to unfold with a written systematic description of the IEP team implications of the planned change, the plan to implement planned change, and a clear explanation of what is required by IEP team members during and after the change procedure. In almost all cases, the change attributes will be implementation of part II.

Change objectives are established by either IEP team members or an ad hoc committee of the team members. Change objectives could include statements such as, "Team members will demonstrate reporting of assessment results to the IEP team in a concise and meaningful delivery," or "Parents will have knowledge of how to report a 'parents' assessment' to the IEP team."

These examples will specifically identify the means to IEP team change, or school or district change. The objectives help coordinate and direct the initiation and the methods to implement systemic change to ascertain success.

Intervention

Group decisions are the keystone to the planned change supporting the learning organization. Intervention is the action taken to demonstrate attainment of goals and objectives that are the responsibility of the entire team. Three steps to the intervention appear necessary for this IEP team: problem solving, use of best practices, and aligning experimentation to organizational knowledge.

Problem solving is the first step in developing learning organization intervention plans. The team should ask, "What is it we want to change and what do we want to accomplish?" These questions will ultimately lead to problems in reaching the desired outcomes. The team will then want to analyze the problems and look for gaps between current practice and the desired state. The team will then have observable and defined issues to plan solutions.

Best practices are sought through literature, other teams, and districts. Through this process of asking what is working and what results have been gained from other attempts to implement solutions to great IEP teams, the IEP team can objectively assess gaps, missed opportunities, and mistakes as well as see new ideas at work. Without grounding in best practices, team efforts are generally pure guesswork and hypothetical attempts resulting in failed initiatives.

Alignment of experimental with organizational knowledge is an ongoing process of reviewing what has been done in the past and using the benefits and weaknesses of previous operations to meld into strategies for the future. Knowledge from understanding the history of right and wrong of past events offers insight into how future experiences may relate to the manner in which new initiatives are formed and developed.

All members of the team should be involved in this step, because knowledge to be aligned with new ideas must be understood by all. Ideas, benchmarks, and experimentation do not belong to only one or few members responsible for the information, but in a learning organization the information belongs to all. The transfer of knowledge is essential.

Evaluation

This last step of the planned change process is the measurement of satisfaction with the changes produced by the intervention. The team again must ask two questions: "What changes are readily seen by the planned change, and were all members and other stakeholders satisfied with the changes?" Answers to these questions may be formed through an analysis of organization cultural gaps and fits.

The team would consider the underlying norms, values, and beliefs that were presented by the change results, and the team would analyze the team and organizational artifacts produced by the planned change. Data collected from these perspectives would be aligned to the gap and fit analysis to direct future movement and quality improvement of the team.

In conclusion, the movement of an IEP team to accept and implement a new way to conduct IEP meetings needs to be directed by a transformational leader and a plan. By following the simpler plan of developing the plan, selling it, and modifying, the plan can be successful and fulfilling. The six-step process described by Armenakis et al. is important to understand as a process to plan on a large scale. However, the engagement of an IEP team can be rather informal, direct, and easily implemented on a small scale.

The snowball effect will take place as different members of the IEP team spread out into other IEP team meetings. Parent and student training, discussed in chapter 12, is key, as is the commitment of the transformational leader to move planned change from one small team to another and then school wide. However, as each IEP team accepts change as a norm and a daily practice, new teams signing on will find it easier to work toward producing great IEPs.

ANALYSIS

1. How should a learning organization framework be developed for an individual IEP team?
2. Why is it important to understand the theoretical aspects of planned change to develop a learning organization within the IEP team?
3. What can you do, as team chair and transformational leader, to develop a planned change for your team and your school, and still have significant impact on your district?

EVALUATION

1. What can you do as a nonpositional leader to initiate a learning-organization construct with the IEP team?

2. What gaps do you immediately see in analyzing a planned change for the IEP team?
3. How do you think gaps may be fitted into the team's culture and theories-in-use?
4. What are your fears in thinking about planned change?
5. Do you see other steps that need to be included in the planned change construct to better fit your team's initiative striving toward greatness?
6. How will you present information about a change process to your IEP team?
7. What values and beliefs do you hold as a transformational leader to support an initiative toward a learning environment?

Part III Summary

While much work has been done to convey and interrupt the laws surrounding the IEP team and its duties, little has been done to capture the essence of the law. Part III has attempted to bring forth the spirit of the original law, P.L. 94-142, and all subsequent revisions to ensure that a free and appropriate education is indeed available to all students. This is the spirit of IDEA: the cooperation and collaboration of all interested persons in a child's life.

As stated in the introduction, following the sequence of tasks as described in the preceding chapters will be time consuming and difficult in many ways. But it gets easier. As the district frames its values and culture as a way to engage parents, students, teachers, and administrators into a process of really understanding student outcomes, IEP team meetings become productive, friendly, and actually will save time and resources. Using this model keeps IEP team meetings, including three-year IEPs, to sixty to ninety minutes at the most.

School staff, students, and parents should be prepared to thoroughly know what to expect from each other and themselves. The work to get to this point is worth it. When the entire IEP team is functionally operated by the spirit of the special education laws, great IEPs become an organizational norm—even an organization of the IEP team.

When leaders govern special education services by the spirit of the law and are not necessarily driven by the letter of the law, the result is compliant with the law. Such efforts have far exceeded the minimum standards set by IDEA. The transformational leader has developed a culture of using the special education law to grow from, instead of just meeting the least of requirements. All meeting minimum requirements does is do what is necessary to avoid trouble with the state and the feds.

When the transformational leader understands the spirit of the law, the leader and the IEP team become creative, challenged, and try to find the very best way to deliver optimum services to our valued children and students. These optimum services are purposeful and meaningful to the student, family, school, and adult supports in the future.

When the transformational leader feels this way, the IEP team becomes part of the spirit of the law. The team will make legitimate and personal differences in the lives of persons you are connected with in school, at home, and engaged with in the community at large.

Appendix A

Relationship of the Learning Organization to Transformational Leadership

This writing will describe the nature and overview of two important concepts projected in the three parts of this book: that of the learning organization and of transformational leadership. Both constructs are key for planned change and continuous quality improvements. This appendix was provided to assist the leader in further understanding the concepts presented in parts I and III. First a primer to the learning organization will be presented followed by a description of leadership theory and the movement toward transformational leadership.

THE LEARNING ORGANIZATION

On first impression one would have little difficulty making naïve assumptions that learning organization is good and contemporary transformational leadership promotes a learning organization environment. The literature and practice on learning organization and leadership theory strengthened these assumptions of cozy ideas by using similar terms to justify the human connectedness of leadership functions and the learning organization concepts to what was good for the people in and out of the organizational boundaries.

Terms such as *shared vision* (Senge, 1990); *team work groups* (Bennis and Biedermann, 1997); *shared leadership* (McGill and Slocum, 1994); and *self-managed work teams* (Rost, 1991), as well as a plethora of other 1990 and 2000 terms relating to ways of making workers feel good about their job functions, proliferate leadership theory and organizational learning writings. These terms will probably be contemporary themes in leadership discourse and learning organization implementation in all types of organizations, public-private, large and small, well into the future.

The sharing of terminology created a natural connection of learning organization concept with leadership theory, and on the surface presented a general aura of employee comfortableness, consideration, and concern. It simply looked natural and nice. However, the integration of learning organizational concepts and the theory of transformational leadership may not enjoy a natural interaction or alignment, but one that presents opposing forces of purpose and tension between outcomes.

CONCEPT OF LEARNING ORGANIZATION

It is not very often that word reversal causes much difference or confusion, but this was true when the concepts of learning organization and organizational learning were used either interchangeably or within a similar construct. However, the difference is significant. Argyris (1994) defined *organizational learning* as the "detection and correction of errors" (p. 8). By this definition, Argyris stated organizations learn by agents (employees) learning on their own and contributing back to the organization.

Schein (1996) stated *organizational learning* was the learning by individuals and groups in organizations. In contrast, the *learning organization* was learning by the organization in a system as a whole (Schein, 2010). Senge (1990) provided detail to the learning organization by describing the learning organization as a group of people in an organization building on the ability to create what the group wants to create.

McGill and Slocum (1994) classified traditional organization models as the "knowing organization." This was the organization operated under and by procedures, policies, and rules. The knowing organization was characterized by the belief of knowing the best and only way to do the job. The role of management in the knowing organization was control of employee behavior by the enforcement of the regulations and rules that contributed to the perceived best way to complete the job.

The knowing organization improved only when necessary and through the implementation of new rules and procedures. McGill and Slocum contend the learning organization movement came from the inability of the knowledge organization to effectively operate when real change was required and as job functions became more specialized and complicated.

Several theories and constructs were developed to prepare organizations for the anticipated changes resulting from globalization of business and industry and the rapid growth of information technology. While the concept of learning organization remained confounding and confusing, it may best be actualized not by theory alone, but within a context of elements necessary for an organization to develop an appreciation for learning organization: culture, communication, and community.

Theories of Learning Organizations

Lewin's (1958) Three Stage Change Theory framed one of the original concepts of learning organizations. According to Lewin, anything that was changing within an organization resulted from the direction of an opposing field, as organizations attempted to maintain equilibrium—the status quo. Planned change must counteract the opposing forces of the status quo through the development of action plans to move the equilibrium point in the direction of the planned change.

The action plan moved the point of equilibrium through a three-stage change process of "unfreezing" old behaviors, moving to a new level of organization and employee behaviors, and "refreezing" the new behavior. Lewin's change model postulated change through three levels: changing the individual's skills and values, changing organizational structures and systems, and changing the organizational climate and interpersonal style of the organization.

Argyris and Schön (1974) developed a system of learning in organizational structure as learning occurred in two different models. Model I learning, or single-loop learning (see figure A.1), was a reaction from threat or embarrassment or a continual return to organization structure such as policies and procedures or adapting work methods to meet current situations.

Model II, or double-loop learning (see figure A.2), relied on the learning process to assess at a time of an observed mismatch of desired actions. The learning process involves agents (employees) to review the learning organization's basic beliefs and governing values. This return to the essential existence of the learning loop replaced reaction and response to stimuli found in Model I learning. Often single-loop learning only will fix the surface of a problem, whereas double-loop learning gets to the core of the problem and the organization is able to learn from the repair and the solution. This is often not likely in single-loop learning.

Figure A.1.   Single-loop learning.

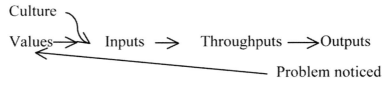

Figure A.2. **Double-loop learning.**

Schein (1994) [Au: add to references] postulated that learning organization was contingent upon an alignment of functions within an organization. Schein reported that all organizations innately maintain three levels of function: (a) operational, (b) technological, and (c) executive. The misunderstanding of the interactions and operations at each and between different levels inhibits development of the learning organization.

Operational functions were where the actual work was manipulated or done. At this level work typically followed prescribed methods of work completion and standards were established for quality and quantity. Workers knew what the procedures were but often developed their own methods to complete work. Work procedures were also changed especially when challenging or threatening situations were presented, or when work became not routine.

The technological level included engineers and information service employees whose function was to optimize technology within the overall organizational function. Many leaders felt this function relied on the premise that technology could do more work at greater efficiency than humans.

The executive levels in organizations were most concerned with the finances of the organization. Schein acknowledged most CEOs move into the executive positions from the technological ranks, but adapt their primary function from technological standards to fiscal matters. This adaptation usually creates organizational misunderstanding.

The misunderstanding occurred as technology devalued the human qualities of operational workers, and the executive level misunderstood operational workers holding the organization back from quality and quantity quotas. Operational workers did not relate to either the technological or executive levels because these levels did not understand the skills necessary to complete work or realize the adaptations that occurred during typical and atypical work periods.

The technology level understood the operational worker as an unnecessary function, since machines and technology could do more work without mistakes for longer periods of time. While the executive level held this same attitude, the executives understood all levels of work as a cost center. Hence any attempt for development of the concept of a learning organization fell into disregard.

Senge (1990) characterized a learning organization as one that embedded knowledge, was interdependent, and had the human communication networks necessary to achieve organizational purpose. Senge described five disciplines of the learning organization as systems thinking, personal mastery, mental models, shared vision, and team learning. Learning organizations continuously worked to develop the five disciplines.

Senge described the learning organization as "where people continually expand their capacity to create the results they truly desire, where new and expansive patterns of thinking are nurtured, where collective aspiration is set free, and where people are continually learning how to learn together" (Senge, 1990, p. 3). The five disciplines did not provide new knowledge as a specialized activity, but as a new behavior of the organization and a way of existence for the agent (employees).

IMPLICATIONS FOR LEARNING ORGANIZATION CONCEPT

Disagreement defining learning organization has led to confusion about how to develop or create a learning organization. Argyris and Schön (1996) indicated there were few examples of practicing learning organizations fully utilizing Model II, double-loop learning. Schein (1996) reported learning barriers and defensive obstacles inhibit learning organization at all levels and in all organizations. The context of learning organizations consists of three aspects (a) culture, (b) communication, and (c) community.

Culture

Practices have demonstrated that learning organizations are engaged with generative learning and have in common a concern for people and an equal concern for all stakeholders. Less obvious, but suggested in theories of learning organizations, is that employees can and do learn, they value learning, and organizations can change for the betterment of persons and structure.

The organizational culture often explained why organizations do not learn. The organizations that became functional learning organizations demonstrated a shared commitment to open and extensive communication, shared commitment to systematic learning and thinking, and shared beliefs of teams and teamwork.

The role of learning organization culture drives the ability of organizations to promote learning. The culture of organizations created the climate for workers to engage in learning. Such organizational culture indicated learning had to be modeled to the worker or member, and organizational culture must accept learning in a risk-free environment for people to re-create the empowerment of personal values.

The greatest inhibitor of learning in the organizational culture was fear. Two types of fear or anxiety had a direct relationship on organizational learning. First were the fear of learning something new, a fear of the unknown, and a fear of a seasoned employee being able to learn new ways. Second was the fear of a worker who must change and learn new things, in order to survive and maintain current status. This inhibitor to learning is based upon being forced to learn to keep the job and a sense of what the employee has been doing is no longer what will be done in the organization.

Learning organization culture must abate the fear of employees needing to survive by the strength of learning new ways as a positive benefit for the employee. Schein (2010) suggested organizational culture must (a) provide psychological safety to initiate the learning process and compete with the employee's fear of the unknown, (b) promote a better vision for the future to reinforce employee and organizational learning in the present, (c) provide places for practice and encourage practice within the organization, and (d) provide leadership, guidance, coaching, and learner reinforcement for small accomplishments. The most important factor of cultural facilitation was providing an environment that acknowledged mistakes and errors as an integral force of the learning process.

The cultural impact on learning may be less difficult with a flatter organizational structure. A flatter structure is important when systems of information are producing fast and massive feedback to the organization, with increased experimental learning and continuous knowledge requirements. The management of culture to improve organizational learning processes when organizations are faced with the aforementioned situations is key to a learning organization.

Communication

All learning organizations understand through cultural perceptions and operational interpretations that the organization and the larger environment must embellish communication. The perceptions and interpretations of learning organizations usually are developed by enriched relationships generated through all levels of employee communication.

Such a method of communication defined the structure and adapted the environment to include strategic choices, theory and skills, and defining of roles and processes of the organization. Learning organizations were considered generative organizations as verbal systems exhibited by the use of stories of organizational history, metaphors of organizational values, and the way organizations explore learning.

The organizations that were exercising global communication emphasizing trust, values, and history were ready to meet the dynamic demands of a changing environment. Effective learning organizations create a greater sense of connectedness between all levels of the organization than traditional organizations. Verbal, nonverbal, and written communication also reinforce openness, truth, and performance. The best method to create communicative connectedness was through open dialogue.

As discussed earlier, Schein (1996) described three levels of organizational culture: the operational level (line workers and people who do hands-on work), technology level (engineers and information systems), and executive level (CEOs and presidents). A natural mismatch of understanding between these levels created cultural and communicative misunderstanding. One method to harmonize mutual understanding between the three diffused levels was an open line of communication built between workers at all levels to appreciate and accept the perspective of each. Through communication, an integrated view of the organization was possible and learning could occur.

Effective communication explored the diversity as a polyphonic organization and plurality between people in the ways members understood differing attitudes: by using words. The communicative learning organization was one that existed as a socially constructed verbal system of text, stories, and discourse. In the polyphonic organization every member had a voice. Some were loud and others quiet, but the organization recognized each voice as being the center of each person's own organization.

The communicative learning organization was congruent to Senge's view of the powerlessness and unworthiness found when members started to develop personal mastery. The learning organization in Senge's view advocated the development of individual vision to understand the workers' current reality to gain personal mastery while overcoming powerlessness and unworthiness. When personal mastery was shared with others, a notion of shared vision was invested in the community of others.

Community

Community was the understanding of organizational wholeness. Many organizations attempting to transform or begin systemic change partialized the organization and highlighted departments or functions within the system. Senge (1990) stated, "Living systems have integrity" (p. 66). While many organizational problems might not be understood by looking at the whole, most change was effective when the organization was not divided into smaller units.

However, subsystems, like the IEP team, were seen as an effective mechanism or starting place to engage the whole. This is where the IEP team fits into community as the initial boost to develop culture, communication, and community. The issues of foregoing community existed when the IEP team stopped at this entry point as an independent subsystem.

It will be important to realize that starting with an IEP team is important to grow the system. Working in this manner is not partializing the independence of the planned change, but moving slowly as the subsystem gains momentum and corrects errors.

There exists an analytic perspective that breaks organizational or operational parts into individual processes. This analytical perspective separated whole systems into units; each unit was analyzed in isolation of other parts, and the divided units were reassembled. When subsystems are the total focus, the IEP team in isolation may demonstrate significant limitations when the team efforts leave the larger system out of the community of the learning organization. Systems required understanding how each unit fit into the larger system, as parts could not be taken as a primary factor of analysis.

Senge (1990) referred to the Indivisible Whole as a characterization of the fifth discipline of a learning organization. The Indivisible Whole recognized there were no separations, gaps, and boundaries in the organization. Systems operated only as a whole, while division of the whole weakened the overall purpose of the organization. Senge felt this was likewise true for learning organizations.

Leaders should identify with the whole and not isolate parts only to lose sight of the system itself. However, starting with one IEP team does not isolate that team from the realm of special education services or the student from other students. Isolation would divide the whole system, forcing organizations to fix a small part when usually the larger system needs to change. Fixing a part only postpones what really needs to be done.

Fragmentation will not work in a technological age where systems were global, multidimensional, and fluid. Learning organizations must begin viewing the world as a whole within a whole, not the world as parts that formed wholes. Learning organizations began in some place, such as the IEP team, within an organization and may, given successful variables, expand into the larger organizational system. The learning organization was a process; it grew and it matured. This process explained the difference from the organization that fragments and divides wholes into *smaller units, forgoing any understanding of how to put the units back together.*

BARRIERS TO LEARNING ORGANIZATION CONCEPT

While the learning organization was the outcome of effective planned organizational change, the learning organization concept is complex. Learning generally occurred at the individual level, and organizations learn from the employees and stakeholders. However, organizations represent a system consisting of employees, inventory, resources, and processes.

The system is not always geared for learning and change. The anxiety of learning within a system created levels of anxiety that overwhelm any benefit from learning.

Fragmented learning occurred when individuals learn parts and not the whole, or learn new knowledge but do not contribute the knowledge to the organization. Another threat to learning was opportunity learning. Opportunity learning occurred as employees used knowledge to gain control and power, and while the knowledge could have value to the organization, it had no influence to or on the organization.

Organizational structure inhibited learning as divisions and work functions became more specialized and discrete. Learning occurred within subgroups, but not within the broader system of the organization. Organizations experienced individual learning occurring at different levels, with different employees, and in different groups; the learning was not coordinated and therefore did not affect the organization. Such maneuvering could cause separation in large systems, and learning was used to protect subunits and resource tools for future influence.

Covert and power maneuvering, hierarchical structure, and fear of change inhibited learning organization concepts from developing. The words used to characterize learning organization were generally words many individuals found difficult to grasp, especially during times of change, fear, or anxiety.

The introduction of learning organization, like leadership, needed to reify its existence. For many, it was believed that a learning organization would never reach an ultimate place; the position will always be changing. Its existence is characterized by the attributes of a learning organization as a strategic intent to learn, an organization facilitating learning, systems that promote an open culture, and learning from others.

THEORIES OF LEADERSHIP

Theories of leadership provided the range of thoughts far wider than the concepts found in learning organization. Perhaps because the notion of leadership has spanned many more years and perhaps because the concept of leadership had a wider public appeal, the theories of leadership exhibited a massive spectrum of ideas.

Until Burns (1978) theorized the birth of transformational leadership, early pundits described leadership as a position or a title in an organization. The characteristics and traits of leaders were seen by respected persons, by situations demanding leadership, and by exchange and contingency actions to motivate or control workers.

All of the early theories of leadership led to the perception that leadership was power, and power was a result of getting people to do what they normally would not do. Leadership managed business and government to accomplish new things of importance to the leader. Burns changed the perception and laid new foundations for a new style of leadership as he categorized leadership as either transactional or transformative.

Transactional leadership was based on the exchange between the leader and follower. Transactional leadership was based on fairness, honesty, loyalty, and integrity. Transactional leadership was also characterized as "immobilizing, self-absorbing, and eventually manipulative" (Ciulla, 1998, p. 113). Transactional leadership attempted to gain control of followers by reaching out to their lowest level of human and employee needs.

Burns described the second category of leadership as transformational, a belief that leadership encouraged leaders and followers to see a new social environment. This leadership encouraged leaders and followers to change together, seeking new concerns for the human condition. Transformational leadership attempted to unite leader and follower to pursue common aspirations, by elevating member values to higher beliefs. The transformation goal of leadership was mutual between organization and employees displaying values of liberty, justice, and equality.

Transformational leadership introduced the concept that leadership and position were not synonymous. Transformational leadership was a reciprocal process to mobilize all members with mutual values and goals. This process had impact on the structure of organizations when transformational leadership was evidenced. Mutual understanding reduced the reliance on hierarchical frameworks of organization as leadership transcended through all levels of the structure.

Mutual understanding between leaders and followers was a necessary component for change. When leadership was associated with formal position, the complexity of organization disregarded mutual understanding and the methods to promote meaningful change.

Transformational leaders were people who had the capacity to mobilize others and elevate their peers. Burns stated leaders must have the ability to think and feel as fully capable persons and not be trapped in narrow-mindedness or self-appointed importance. Burns (1978) summarized, "the grand goal of leadership—to help create or maintain social harbors for personal islands" (p. 449).

Transformational leadership was mutual understanding, and the concept of leadership was a community—neighbors of leaders and followers with equal responsibility for leadership. The ideals of transformational leadership encouraged active participation of followers. When followers and leaders were active participants, change developed to transform mutual purpose.

Transformational leadership with active participants sought transformation, and leadership happened throughout all organizational structure to effectively motivate all participants toward change.

LEADERSHIP THEORY TO SUPPORT LEARNING ORGANIZATION

Transformational leaders enabled employees to find meaning and fulfillment transforming fundamental attitudes, values, and commitments. This transformation potentially established higher goals and greater purpose as members gained independence and autonomy. Leadership in the learning organization was transformational. Transformational leaders espoused strong beliefs and values of human potential.

Moral issues were important to the transformational leader, and values were highlighted and strengthened by the process of elevating people to confront their own reassessment of values and needs. Burns proposed two moral questions to shape the understanding of transformation: What was the moral use of power, and was there tension between the leader's public and private morality?

Greenleaf (1977) stated, "Spirit, not knowledge, is power" (p. 136). This was the guiding principle of servant leadership. Greenleaf explained that spirit was present in the leader being the servant first, ensuring all members' needs were taken care of before the leader's needs were met. Greenleaf's theory focused on those being served, and eventually the followers will understand that spirit will motivate themselves to become servant leaders and serve others.

Greenleaf explained that servant leadership "gives certainty and purpose to others who may have difficulty achieving it for themselves" (p. 15). Servant leadership turned the hierarchical chart upside down—the leader met the needs of the followers and the consumers. This then was community, and the community formed the basis of existence for the organization.

The goal of servant leadership was the outcome of leadership actions on the most vulnerable member of the community. Servant leadership was the means by which leaders have the necessary legitimacy to lead. Servant leadership provided legitimacy because the responsibilities of leadership were to give a sense of direction and to establish an encompassing and meaningful purpose.

Sergiovanni (1992) introduced moral leadership into leadership theory with the concepts of purposing and covenant building. The concept of purposing was a five-step process to transfer core values to organizational practice. Core values were the moral principles defined by an organization that ensured equal treatment and respect for the integrity of all members, and concern for the welfare of the organization as a community.

Through this process, core values were clearly and frequently communicated to all stakeholders in and outside the organization. The core values facilitated decision making and guided final recommendations. Leadership generated resources to support the core values and ensured that core values generalize throughout the organization. Outcomes of moral leadership supported core values through everyday actions and enforcing practices that exemplified core values.

The concept of covenant building provided a morally based contractual relationship bonding persons together through membership connections. Such relationships offered meaning in the work lives of members and provided reciprocal rights, duties, and obligations to define guidelines for action. Covenant building and purposing assisted organizations in reaching their full potential.

LEADERSHIP IMPLICATIONS FOR
LEARNING ORGANIZATIONAL CONCEPTS

Argyris (1994) presented the primordial factor of leadership of the learning organization developing single and double-loop learning. Schein (2010) =referred to these learning styles as adaptive and generative learning. Adaptive learning focused on solving problems or mismatches of organizational purpose by fixing the present and apparent condition causing the mismatch. The organization adapted change from the assumed cause of the mismatch.

Generative learning or double-loop learning questioned the fundamental values and beliefs of the organization guiding the ways of problem solving, decision making, and engaging in organizational planning (Argyris, 1994). Generative learning was a possibility through transformational leadership.

Leadership assumed a different function in structures developing learning organization concepts than those organizations grounded in traditional styles and practices. Transformational leaders that create learning organizations were actually building new organizations, organizations that provided opportunities for members to expand capabilities to shape the future. The outcome of building learning organization was an organization leading itself with the moral fortitude to meaningfully meet society's needs.

Developing an organization with abilities to enrich culture and enhance communication and understanding wholeness of organizational existence required patience, vision, and courage. Leadership in a learning organization was an undefined role, one that set aside traditional views of leadership and espoused a new view of leadership by centering on vision and compassion. Senge described three critical roles of leaders in the learning organization: designers, stewards, and teachers.

The leader as designer was the leader who created culture-supporting learning. The environment of the learning organization was one that understood error as a learning tool, encouraged risk taking, permitted practice of skills, and supported team development of concepts and ideas. Leaders who cared and had a vision for cohesive design and teamwork, while generating efficient and effective work patterns, created the learning organization.

The learning organization defined by Senge was founded on the five disciplines (systems thinking, personal mastery, mental models, shared vision, and team learning), and learning organizations demanded leadership to initiate the process of learning. The move from adaptive learning to generative learning required a facilitating leader to design a learning culture.

The leader as steward was the one who developed a unique relationship to build learning organizations with the leader's personal vision. The leader became the steward of this vision. The visionary leader viewed learning as a creation of deeper understanding and purpose, and the learning organization had a responsibility to the structure and humankind.

The transformational leader was considered in learning organizations as servant leadership. Building learning organizations and individual capabilities by the transformational leader must be collective, and collective leadership systematically cycled as followers began to lead themselves. The designer leader invested energy and took the risks to inspire others with a vision of the future. This vision must be communicated to followers through words and deeds so every worker understood the purpose to instinctually motivate and move persons and organizations forward toward the vision.

Communication was a critical force for effective learning organizations and for leadership to dispel the expected fear and anxiety associated with learning among workers. Learning occurred as a result of the communication between people, and verbal interactions occurred because leadership desired learning.

The leader as teacher conceived the existence of the organization as one piece and ensured units of the organization did not stray from the whole. Teaching was a primordial attribute of leadership, as teaching helped persons understand an accurate, insightful, and empowering view of reality. Reality was the realm in which the organization survived.

When executives attempted to implement fragmented policies and strategies, learning became fragmented and disconnected from the purpose of the organization. The organization and all its parts must be considered as one, and teaching viewed process and content as inseparable. Subsystems, like an IEP team, may start a teaching and learning effort toward the learning organization, but at a point the larger system, or the school or district, will need to come together.

The leader as teacher helped the worker learn wholeness through the integration of work units. The leader modeled concepts of learning as a process, and the teacher empowered learners to think deeply of the purpose and existence of themselves and others, in and out of the organization.

Leadership in a learning organization is a significant departure from the traditional concept of the leader. The traditional perception of the leader has been changed due to learning organization concepts of generative learning and transformational leadership. The leader must not only have to ascribe to a transformational leadership theory, but express attributes of leadership far differently than traditional leadership characteristics.

The attributes necessary for new leadership included communication skills, negotiation skills, motivational skills, change management skills, empowerment skills, and a vision for the future.

Transformational leadership in learning organizations ensured the continuing presence of beliefs of the learning culture. Leadership exhibited organizational concern for people in the form of equal opportunity of all stakeholders. Equal concern meant sharing organizational values and believing the members can and will learn.

Leadership ensured a shared belief that the surrounding culture, and the world, could be changed, and culture and world changes result from the shared commitment to think systemically. Leadership must ensure that open and extensive communication existed in order for persons and teams to effect large and broad change.

Leadership acknowledging how deeply the leader's individual perceptions, thoughts, and feeling had been acculturated must break through mature and strongly perceived organizational cultures. Awareness of the leader's cultural assumptions was essential to learn the attributes of and change to an entirely new organizational culture, the learning organization.

The learning organization will challenge leadership in the developing learning organization, as learning organization will not occur within traditional hierarchical structures. Significant change required imagination, perseverance, dialogue, deep caring, and a willingness to change. In developing learning organizations, the key to leadership was to express experience not as how learning occurred as a process, but how experience had bound learning and what skills the learner possessed.

DO LEARNING ORGANIZATION AND TRANSFORMATIONAL LEADERSHIP HAVE AN IMPACT?

Sheppard and Brown (2000) conducted a two-year research study of nine schools in a district to determine if learning organization concepts would be implemented following extensive leadership training. Leaders of the nine schools participated in a five-day institute on building learning schools. The training included developing the learning organization, strategies for developing the learning organization, team leadership, group decision making, accountability in the learning organization, action research for growth and improvement, and implementation model combining action research and change theory. Following the institute, the leaders were to implement learning organization concepts in the local schools. The local university conducting the research provided follow-along technical assistance. The schools were asked to engage action research on student outcomes, school structure, leadership, professional training, and classroom practices.

Each school made a commitment to engage in the action research and implement learning organization concepts. Findings of this study suggested there were connections between leadership and the development of learning organization and classroom practices. However, the process was difficult, and several important conditions were present during the two-year research.

Time to implement changes by the teaching staff was restricted to before- and after-class times. The teachers felt distrust of the leadership, as it appeared this learning organization project was one more thing teachers were forced to do. Leaders expressed there was little time for team building and sharing leadership. Teachers and leaders felt interference from the district as teachers and leaders were instructed to develop individual initiatives while the district limited actions to those consistent with the district's vision.

Personnel changes severely disrupted team constituency and team development and may have had an effect on apathy toward change. Apathy was also noted by the continual presence of many educational innovations, and this project was just another. Budget constraints reduced future professional development opportunities. Several schools experienced an unwillingness of the administrators to share power, reinforcing the traditional organizational structure.

The findings in the Sheppard and Brown study were consistent with the concerns expressed by Schein (2010) describing inhibitions of cultural development and organizational learning. Schein was concerned that hierarchical, traditional structure was the only organization that most persons were familiar with, and the only one used predominantly in the United States.

Schein projected managers would always need to be in control by being decisive and dominant, while expressing that they do not need to learn, as managers already have all the answers. The perception of leader was the rugged individual—the hero—albeit teams and flatter organizations did not have heroes. Work tasks remain largely compartmentalized, and hierarchy was the main source of security and status, while task issues were projected as more important than relationship issues. Finally, management does not deal with soft things. Creating a learning culture with this set of inhibitors was difficult and probably impossible.

THE CHALLENGE

The concept of centralized leadership characterized by traditional structure and established practices will likely be replaced in the near future with centered leaders who participate freely within the chaotic generative organizations organized for persistent and constant change. Despite the softness of the learning organization environment and the ease leaders may have labeling their organization as a learning culture, the evolving learning organization will be a rigorous challenge for all school personnel and education stakeholders.

The excitement, fear, and confusion of newer educational models proliferate throughout the academic spectrum: charter schools, response to intervention, differentiated learning, and learning communities are just a few of the potentially significant advances bolstering education. These changes are necessary, for education was hovering over the same tried and true but not inclusive or results-driven paradigms for a long time.

True, it seems like a lot is coming at one time, but if special educators can get hold of really leading the IEP team, incorporating attributes of the learning organization and transformational leadership, then positive movement toward inclusiveness and integration of all students can most likely become a reality.

This reality will change school, district, and even the little IEP team toward a new culture consisting of new beliefs and values. These new values and beliefs will drive espoused theory to theories-in-use demonstrating new daily and ongoing practices to ensure every student has a great opportunity to achieve and perform skills leading to a successful life and a bigger world picture.

To develop the learning organization within the IEP team requires redesign in how leaders think and what leaders believe. Unless there is a deep and personal commitment by IEP leaders and followers, efforts to create a learning organization will be predestined to the ranks of a failed passing thought. When personal commitment is made to the learning organization concept and transformational leadership by the leader as well as team members, GREAT things can happen.

Appendix B

Samples of a Student Curriculum for Students to Participate in Their IEP Team Meeting

NEED

Many students receiving special education services do not actively participate in their IEP team meeting or have had limited experience and no preparation to engage in this meeting. Few students ever assist in the development of goals and supports included in their IEP. In many cases students do not know what to do during the meeting or have not had any guidance to understand the roles and input they can provide during the IEP team meeting.

PURPOSE

This curriculum has been outlined to help students (and sometimes parents and teachers) to know how to present meaningful and relevant information to the IEP team. Additionally the student will understand that the student is an equal and an essential member of the IEP team.

MODIFICATIONS

Modifications will obviously need to be made to accommodate student abilities and capacities. The presented plan is organized as a model and one that will need to be flexed individually for each student. The content and the outcomes should remain as presented, but methodology and supports require adaptations depending upon student needs.

TEACHING ENVIRONMENT

It is expected that teaching the student how to gainfully participate at his or her own IEP team meeting will occur at school and at home. Throughout this writing emphasis has been placed on parents and students becoming actively engaged in the IEP process. Therefore students need to be engaged, and this curriculum with appropriate modifications should be presented to the student at school, at home, and in the community.

CURRICULUM ORGANIZATION

This student preparedness for the IEP team meeting curriculum is organized to be modified and adapted according to the individual needs of the student. There are seven domain areas that are appropriate for all students receiving special education services: (a) current academics, (b) cocurricular and personal interests, (c) what has recently been learned and how these new skills are being used in normative living, (d) what student hopes and dreams for the future are, (e) what the student likes to do at school, at home, and in the community, and (f) what the student disagrees with and wants to change (self-advocacy) about the student's educational plan.

Outcomes are developed for each domain area that are appropriate for all students receiving special education services. Outcomes will be identified and specific to the three environments of school, home, and community. Objectives for learning will be presented to support the acquisition of the outcome in each specific environment.

Objectives are to be modified and adapted with appropriate supports and accommodations to match student skills and needs. The learning objectives will generally guide the methodology and the presentation of various skills necessary for the student to participate as fully as possible in IEP team meetings.

Methodology will be presented in a general sense for each objective for use at home and at school. Community environments are best taught through the parents during naturally occurring events and activities. However, there are many opportunities for school to become very actively involved with outcomes applied in the community.

Methodology is dependent upon student learning styles and previous experiences. Methodology should be based upon preferred styles of learning, past experiences, and exposure to previous IEP team meetings and the capacity the student has to self-advocate.

Supports need to be made available to the student when necessary. All teachers know that degrees of support should match the capacity of the student: the Three Bears metaphor—not too much or too little, but just right. Supports, however, need to be considered before starting a teaching sequence. Supports may be different in the three environments and between parents and teachers. Do not think that in school the student just needs a verbal cue and this will be true in all situations. In the community the child may need to have written cues as well as verbal cues.

The last area of this curriculum is evidence that the learning objective is being met. There must be realistic and observable criteria established for each learning objective. This is established to assess if the methodology, supports, and learning styles are all working to attain mastery of the objective and eventually the outcome.

SAMPLE CURRICULUM

Teaching Students to Actively Participate in Their IEP Team Meeting

Domain area: Current academic activities
Outcome at school: The student will express progress being made in content-area subjects to the IEP team at each IEP team meeting.

Objective: When asked by the IEP chair, the student will provide to the IEP team what classes the student is taking and how well the student feels progress is being made from a prepared list of classes and teacher-assisted progress report.

Methodology: Small group instruction, one-on-one to complete list and progress report.

Support: Teacher assistance to prepare list and progress report, notes and verbal cues to present to team.

Evidence of learning: Teacher offers verbal cues during team meeting seven (7) or fewer times to student.

Objective: When asked by the chair of the IEP team, the student will present a concise report of academic progress from a prepared report written by the student with assistance from the teacher.

Methodology: Small group instruction and small group activity to mimic an IEP team meeting in the classroom. Teacher one-on-one assistance if necessary.

Support: Teacher assistance to write the report and to offer cue cards for the presentation at team meeting with verbal cues as necessary.

Evidence of learning: Student provides oral report to IEP team with three (3) or fewer verbal cues from teacher.

Objective: The student will give his report to the IEP team as the student input section is identified on the IEP team welcoming, and the student will make spontaneous comments and input throughout the team meeting appropriately.

    Methodology: Student will practice participation in a contrived mock IEP team meeting with other students and school staff.

    Support: None

    Evidence of learning: Student engages freely and appropriately during the entire IEP team meeting as assessed by the special education teacher and the chairperson.

Outcome at home: The student will express to the IEP team progress and degree to which homework is completed at home without verbal cues from parents.

    Objective: The student will prepare a statement with parents of the efforts taken to complete homework assignments at home.

    Methodology: Parents will work with the student at home to prepare an accurate statement. Parents will help the student practice oral presentation.

    Support: Parents will help student write statement of homework completion and offer ideas to present information.

    Evidence of learning: Student will present statement of homework completion with five (5) or fewer cues from parents.

    Objective: The student will independently assess homework assignments completed and indicate to the team how much of the homework the student can do independently.

    Methodology: Parents will review the components of what should be presented and provide time for student to independently prepare for the IEP team meeting.

    Support: None

    Evidence of learning: Report is presented to IEP team independently with meaningful and appropriate information and with no verbal cues or aids.

Outcome in community: The student will be able to report at IEP team meetings how the student is using learned skills in the community and how successful the learning has been to use skills in natural situations.

    Objective: The student will prepare a list of recent community activities and skills he has recently learned to perform independently during the community activity.

    Methodology: Small group work and one-on-one instruction to complete list of community activity skills at school, and time with parents to discuss and write community skill use at home.

    Support: Teacher and parent assistance to recall events and skill utilization. Calendar is used to keep track of major community events and skills used.

Evidence of learning: List is maintained and kept by student and shown to the teacher and parents on request to assess completeness and timeliness.

Objective: The student will independently report to the team how learned skills are being utilized in various aspects of the student's life.

Methodology: Parents and teacher will remind student to prepare for the IEP team meeting and provide time to prepare for the meeting.

Support: Teacher and parent availability for any assistance requested by the student.

Evidence of learning: Student independently presents report of utilization of learned skills in naturally occurring activities to the IEP team with one (1) or fewer cues from parents or teacher.

Domain area: Cocurricular activities and personal interests

Outcome at school: Student is able to report on cocurricular activities engaged by student at school to the IEP team.

Objective: The student with prepared written cues reads to the IEP team what cocurricular activities the student participates in or would like to do.

Methodology: Small group work with a teacher, one-on-one instruction if necessary to complete cue cards.

Support: Teacher assistance to complete the written cue cards, student use of cue cards.

Evidence of learning: Student reads from cue cards report of involvement in cocurricular activities at school with (5) or fewer prompts from teacher.

Objective: The student spontaneously reports on school activities regularly engaged by student.

Methodology: Teacher review of ideas from the student in small group or individually.

Support: Student may require communication device to verbally report.

Evidence of learning: Student provides spontaneous information with one (1) or fewer prompts from teacher.

Outcome at home: Student is able to report to the IEP team interests and hobbies the student enjoys.

Objective: The student with prepared written cues reads to the IEP team what interests and hobby activities the student participates in or would like to do.

Methodology: Parents assist student list hobbies and interests on cue cards.

Support: Parents may need to assist student to prepare cue cards and may elect to prepare visual flip chart to organize statement to IEP team.

Evidence of learning: Student reads from cue cards report of involvement in interests and hobbies with five (5) or fewer prompts from parent.

Objective: The student spontaneously reports on interests and hobbies regularly engaged by student.

Methodology: Parents will practice presentation at home.

Support: Parents will create a flip chart for practice, but will not plan to use the chart for the presentation to the IEP team.

Evidence of learning: Student provides spontaneous information with one (1) or fewer prompts from parent.

Outcome in community: Student is able to report to the IEP team enjoyable activities the student participates in in the community.

Objective: The student with prepared written cues reads to the IEP team what activities the student participates in or would like to do in the community.

Methodology: Parents assist student list activities on cue cards. Parents will also help student think of activities that may be interesting to try.

Support: Parents may need to help student to think of activities to explore in the community and may assist to prepare cue cards to organize statement to IEP team.

Evidence of learning: Student reads from cue cards report of involvement in the community and new ideas to try with five (5) or fewer prompts from parent.

Objective: The student spontaneously reports on community activities regularly engaged by student and those the student would like to do.

Methodology: Parents will practice presentation at home.

Support: Parents will create a flip chart for practice, but will not plan to use the chart for the presentation to the IEP team.

Evidence of learning: Student provides spontaneous information with one (1) or fewer prompts from parent.

Domain area: How newly learned skills are used

Outcome at school: Student will be able to communicate to IEP team how student has used newly acquired skills in school environments.

Objective: Student, with a visual aid, will indicate by pointing to pictures of newly learned skills in the classroom and match to a functional picture of how the student will use the skill.

Methodology: Student will work with the teacher to construct a picturegram of functional activities common to a school environment completed after the student has met criteria for mastery of the functional skill.

Support: Teacher will need to gather magazines and newspapers and assist student to locate pictures to place on picturegram. Teacher will need to provide physical prompts for cutting and pasting pictures on poster.

Evidence of learning: The completed picturegram will be demonstrated at the next IEP team meeting.

Objective: Student will demonstrate newly learned skills in daily activities in the classroom and at school.

Methodology: Teacher practice with student and sign interpreter on reporting to IEP team.

Support: Student will require a sign interpreter to translate sign to IEP team.

Evidence of learning: Student reports of utilization of recently learned skills in school at the IEP team meeting with one (1) or fewer signed prompts from teacher.

Outcome at home: Student will be able to communicate to IEP team how student has used newly acquired skills in naturally occurring family and home situations.

Objective: Student will use an assisted created poster to indicate how new skills are used at home.

Methodology: Parents will assist student to create a poster highlighting student's independence in newly acquired skills now used as part of the student's daily routine.

Support: Parent assistance to create poster, communication of identified new skills.

Evidence of learning: Completed poster is presented at IEP team meeting.

Objective: Student will sign to IEP team how new skills are applied to his daily life.

Methodology: Parents practice signing how new skills have helped student become more independent.

Support: Parent signing.

Evidence of learning: Student reports through a sign interpreter to the IEP team of how newly acquired skills are being used in student's life with one (1) or fewer prompts from parents.

Outcome in community: Student will be able to communicate to IEP team how student has used newly acquired skills in naturally occurring community environments.

Objective: Student will make a chart to indicate how new skills are used during community activities.

Methodology: Parents will assist student to create a chart indicating student's independence with newly acquired skills in and during community activities.

Support: Parent assistance to create chart, communication of identified new skills and new exposure to new activities.

Evidence of learning: Completed chart is presented at IEP team meeting.

Objective: Student will sign to IEP team how new skills are applied to his experiences and exposures in the community.

Methodology: Parents practice signing how new skills have helped student become more independent in the community and to explore new activities.

Support: Parent signing.

Evidence of learning: Student reports through a sign interpreter to the IEP team how newly acquired skills are being used in the community with one (1) or fewer prompts from parents.

Domain area: Hopes for the future

Outcome at school: Student will be able to express to IEP team personal academic outcomes to achieve student hopes for future postsecondary education or vocational opportunities.

Objective: With assistance from teacher, the student will propose three new skills that the student feels will be important to learn to be successful as an adult.

Methodology: Small group advocacy class, one-on-one teacher-student exploration, visits to postsecondary academic or career institutions.

Supports: Transportation, teacher assistance. Resources from postsecondary options to review.

Evidence of learning: Student will present to the IEP team the three new academic skills thought to be important to student.

Objective: Student will present personal thoughts of skills required to achieve student's hopes for the future.

Methodology: Small group advocacy class, one-on-one teacher-student exploration, visits to postsecondary academic or career institutions.

Supports: Transportation, resources from postsecondary options to review admission requirements, vocational options, support from guidance office and counselor.

Evidence of learning: Student will present to the IEP team an academic plan of skills thought to be important by student.

Outcome at home: Student will be able to express to the IEP team student hopes for independent or supported adult living.

Objective: With parent assistance, the student will discuss living opportunities after K–12 and student will present ideas to IEP team.

Methodology: Parents and students will discuss a range of adult living, vocational, and leisure options, finding some that seem possible and favorable.

Supports: Parent input, visits to different living options, schools, vocational sites.

Evidence of learning: Student and parents will present information and favorable responses to the IEP team.

Outcome in community: Student will be able to express to the IEP team student hopes for socialization and peer relations outside of school as an adult.

Objective: With parent assistance, the student will discuss social opportunities after K–12 and student will present ideas to IEP team.

Methodology: Parents and students will discuss a range of social and relational options, finding some that can be experienced as a teenager.

Supports: Parent input, visits to socialization experiences, increased exposure to new social activities and events.

Evidence of learning: Student and parents will present information and favorable responses to the IEP team.

Domain area: What student likes to do and what student would like to learn to do

Outcome at school and home: Student will be able to express to teachers, parents, and the IEP activities and interests the student likes to do.

Objective: The student will be able to tell parents, teachers, and the IEP team activities and interests the student likes to be engaged with self and others.

Methodology: Teachers and parents should always be ready to listen to ideas from the student. Student will be prompted at appropriate times to express feelings of likes and dislikes. Opportunities will be provided for student to explore new activities.

Supports: Exposure to new events and activities, opportunities to explore new venues and groups, social supports in new situations, rehearsal and practice of handling new social engagements.

Evidence of learning: Student will freely express to parents, teachers, and the IEP team things the student likes to do and new activities the student wants to try.

Domain area: What to change

Outcome: Student knows how to express to others what the student feels is necessary to change regarding the IEP, supports, and opportunities to grow toward a young adult.

> Objective: Student will be able to talk to appropriate persons, teachers and parents for example, about what the student would like to change.
>
>> Methodology: Small group advocacy classes, one-on-one teaching of self-advocacy with counselor discussing how to express a desire to advocate for oneself and functional manners to advocate for change.
>>
>> Support: Teacher and parent assistance to support student in approaching others about a desire to make changes, ideas to help with making an appropriate case to support requested change.
>>
>> Evidence of learning: Student will appropriately request a change of the IEP, supports, or other opportunities or lack thereof with minimal adult assistance.
>
> Objective: The student understands that not everything the student wants to change can change.
>
>> Methodology: Small group advocacy classes, one-on-one teaching of self-advocacy with counselor discussing how to handle requests for change, understanding that the change is not possible, and how to accept the disappointment.
>>
>> Support: Teacher and parent assistance to support student dealing with disappointment.
>>
>> Evidence of learning: Student will appropriately request a change of the IEP and be able to accept request denial in an appropriate and social manner.

This is a model curriculum. Teachers and parents will need to develop an individual plan for a specific student presenting unique capacity and needs. It is important to remember that applying the curriculum in the three environments of school, home, and the community is important.

It is also easy to see that often the objectives, methodology, supports, and evidence of learning are not that different. The three environments and coordination of parents and teachers working together should provide a functional and consistent learning situation for the student.

These skills are extremely important for the learner to have in the student's tool box for successful adult living. We as professionals and we as parents cannot minimize the impact these skills will have in supporting students entering the world of adulthood and helping them become successful and happy.

Appendix C

Application of Business Model to the IEP Team

Throughout this writing the author has mentioned and sometimes written in some detail about the abstract concept described as a learning organization. In a brief and largely unfair summary of the work by Senge (1990) and Argyris (1994) the learning organization was portrayed to reflect growth and quality improvement of a group of people, or a team working toward the same common goal.

Senge's work seems to be rather nonprescriptive, and Argyris appears to purport a system of planned actions. Their work is important to understand, as it forms the basis of the learning organization and the principles of a school in transition or an IEP team desiring positive change.

From these beginnings of a methodical thought and an initial awareness of the need for a group (IEP team), division (school), or an entire organization (district) to appreciate and strive toward improvement through organization change or quality improvement, many other pundits have embraced the basic concepts of a learning organization.

The groundbreaking thesis of Senge and Argyris and others opened a new field of business enterprise: organizational development. Organizational development is an operational side of the theoretical powers of the learning organization as conceived by its founders. The practicality posited by consultants and leaders of organizational development seemed to flip the term of learning organization to a more easily understood term of organizational learning than learning organization. This flip on the surface seems to make little difference, but the guiding tenets are actually far apart and therefore dangerously misguided.

Although the term *organizational learning* appears to have a greater public appeal, the manner in which organization developmental professionals apply the term moves the responsibility of transformation or organizational improvement from the norms and culture of the organization as implied by the learning organization. The organizational learning model seems to place responsibility on the individual worker or stakeholder; learning organization is a systemic model.

THE LEARNING ORGANIZATION

Most business leaders find that implementing a learning organization is difficult, and many decide to hire an organization development consultant to lead the process. In the author's opinion this is where the process begins to fall apart. This is the transformational leader's job. The leader of the organization sets the tone, the example, the values or theories-in-use of the organization, not the consultant. Often it is thought that bringing someone new, a consultant, into the mix is better because the consultant does not have an established and perceived idea of the organization, and additionally the consultant will be fair because there are no expectations coming into the organization. Nonetheless, the consultant is paid through the approval of the leader of the organization!

The learning organization becomes a long-term relationship between all stakeholders of the organization change unit: the district, school, or IEP team. Currently, at the speed of global organizational change, maintaining a status quo is actually moving backward. Change is necessary for sustained existence and for striving toward the organization's mission. Change can be done for the sake of change, or change can be lived as a daily part of the work life or the norm of the organization. The learning organization primarily commences and is sustained with a transformational school leader, not a consultant.

Applying the principles of the learning organization as described by Senge is difficult. His seminal work, *The Fifth Discipline*, is a thesis of ideals and strategies, not explained as an application or as a how-to. To complicate the learning organization even more is its lack of use or even understanding within the education community and school or IEP team environment.

Learning organization is seen as a business model, and generally educators do not put a lot of credibility in business models and strategies. But there are some business principles that make sense within an educational system: learning organization, double-loop learning, and transformational leadership. These models can work well together, and in fact can be put together in transforming the educational organization. Each of the three themes will be discussed separately and then put together as a transforming education organization.

Implementing a learning organization is a stakeholder commitment from the community, the school board, school administrators, teaching and specialist staff, and all nonteaching employees. It just does not start on its own; it builds by discrete planning over time. It is not a flow chart or a time graph that depicts accomplishments by certain dates or a graph of events or deadlines; it is a mindset of re-creating school or IEP team culture and establishing daily norms of operations to reflect the changing IEP team culture.

Learning organization is about learning to do work better and more efficiently and effectively; it is about a safe environment to try new ideas, it is about sharing thoughts and having an avenue to do that without risk. Learning organizations see failure as a learning process, see new ideas as a success, and see time to share thoughts, ideas, and issues as the essence of the learning organization system.

The leader's role is critical. The leader will need to create a safe place for employees and stakeholders to try new ideas and to assist others in the educational processes. The leader will need to open doors for the community to become engaged in what is happening and what should be happening in the district schools, or the IEP team meeting. The leader will have to prove to employees that all ideas are good and will be explored, not necessarily by the leader, but by a team or an appropriate group to assess all ideas.

The leader needs to work as an example that risk and failure are part of the process, that all employees have unique and interesting strengths and weaknesses, that stakeholders all see the educational process differently and not one is wrong or even right, that outside interests and knowledge have a place in the workplace, or time is justified for sharing.

The stakeholders have an interesting role in the learning organization, as they too must be brought along by the leader and hence the culture. There will be criticism. Some will assume this stuff is fluff and therefore a waste of good time; others will maintain that school staff just needs to get on with their job. These attitudes are killers, and the leader must delicately deal immediately with such attitudes and perceptions. Community stakeholders may be the most difficult, since most community stakeholders have a wide variety of opinions and beliefs about education and educational services.

The development of a learning organization in an educational system, either district wide, school, or IEP team, should follow a loosely defined strategic plan. Loosely defined allows the ebb and flow of the organization culture and norms in change mode to be fluid. Fluidity helps to meet the needs of its members and responds appropriately to external changes such as funding, mandates, rules, and internal presentations.

This loosely defined process would include the following components within any formation of the change unit, the subsystem being changed, be it the district, an individual school, a school department, or the IEP team itself: (a) meet for a series of planning sessions with the major stakeholders, (b) devise a method to implement foundation or guiding principles of the learning organization, (c) demonstrate principles to all stakeholders, (d) provide training opportunities for all stakeholders on the critical aspects of change as brought forward by the principles of the learning organization change unit, (e) modify, change, and revamp activities and plans as the learning organization change unit is created by all stakeholders, (f) set up committees to monitor and explore further expansion of learning organization efforts.

The first step is to gather the major stakeholders. On a district level this would include school board members, top administrators, parents, students, and involved community members; for school, major stakeholders may include school board, parents, principals, and a district administrator; and for an IEP team, members who usually participate in most IEP team meetings.

A series of sessions would be held to discuss the theoretical foundations of the learning organization and why this effort should be promoted within the change unit. This step needs to be organized and implemented by the most top-ranking member, who may or may not be a transformational leader. This top-ranking member, however, must have a solid foundation of the theoretical aspects of the learning organization or rely on the transformational leader to take the lead of this project. The leader needs to be knowledgeable of learning organization applications in business and industry, as there are very few solid education examples.

The next step is for this group of top-ranking members or the transformational leader, if not the ranking member, to devise a fluid plan to begin the change process. Fluidity is important as discussed above, but it needs to be structured enough to have credibility with other members. The plan should include steps to train members, a start of a list of activities to promote a culture change, and a do-not-fail commitment.

Topics to be highlighted should involve ways to make participating team members safe in the learning organization environment, such as no retribution for ideas or for failed attempts to change, access to all major stakeholders, and safety in job status and position through the change process. These are difficult bridges to cross, but essential for the learning organization to be successful.

The third step is the "proof in the pudding" step, as now the major stakeholders must prove to all members in the change unit that what was set up in step two is actually what is going to happen—and members must be able to see it happen. This is the time for the "theories-in-use" discussed in chapter 3 to be developed and be very transparent. Any espoused theory will destroy all and any current and future attempts to promote the learning organization.

Members must be able to see that failed attempts at improvement or controversial ideas are rewarded as learning, not as a justification for punishment or maintaining the status quo. Change is always hard, and most employees in a work setting will see change as threatening to employee status or switching up the prevailing methods of working. Doing work differently must be seen as a reinforcing activity, not as punishment, for it to be successful.

Training is the fourth step, and again, the trainer should be one of the major stakeholders. Training must be sincere and supportive, it must be reflective of the needs of change unit members, and the training must be relevant and appropriate to the change unit. Training should be considered as ongoing; a one-hour PowerPoint presentation will not do it! In fact the training should be in smaller groups without the distraction of a lot of technology.

The premise of the learning organization is thought-provoking, emotional, thoughtful, and creative. Generic PowerPoint or other electronic presentations will deter significantly from the message that needs to be delivered.

Small group meetings in which the trainer sits and calmly talks about the culture of the change unit, the reasons for looking at effectiveness, and the impact of change for a very real need of continuous quality improvement brings all members together and even will equalize the status strata—this is obvious with large group, electronically delivered mass training.

The fifth step is to start the process—slowly, but in a real and meaningful way. Change unit members will need to see that the unit is flexible to the changing and developing needs of the school or IEP team members. All reinforcing attributes of the learning organizations must be evident and observable so members will feel safe and in the process. Ideas should be expected, not criticized by anyone anywhere.

Mindsets of stakeholders must be free from preconceived notions of "the old way" to create a fun, exciting, and protected attitude toward this initiative. When new ideas are put into place, the members need to be able to react and respond to the change (even very small change) to let the system permit modification and remediation as appropriate.

Only during the last of the initiation steps does the change unit set up small and open committees to divide and specialize activities and further develop the learning organization. All committees should post meeting times and communicate freely what activities or ideas are being discussed or planned. Meetings are always open, and input from others is welcome. Communication is a key. Because a small change in one area will affect every other part of the change unit and probably the entire system, communication and openness are critical.

DOUBLE-LOOP LEARNING

Double- and single-loop learning (Argyris, 1994) have been known in the business and industry world for some time but rarely considered as a change agent in education systems. Single-loop learning is an attempt to identify the point at which a process appears to falter. The idea of the organization using a single-loop return attacks the problem at the perceived point that the process is not working as smoothly as it should. This single loop attempts to fix the problem at the point of difficulty.

Double-loop learning is a return, not just to the point of where the problem is, because that often does not fix the problem, but back to the basic core values of the organization. As the process is reviewed at the point of difficulty and the point of understanding organization cultural values, the difficult challenges are better able to be fixed or remediated to improve organizational effectiveness.

With the addition of returning to core values and cultural norms, many times employees are able to gain a deeper and richer understanding of the need to change and to see processes differently than as viewed through a single-loop design of remediation.

A double-loop learning process was observed in an elementary school trying to provide teachers an opportunity to meet and share ideas for improving the coordination of instruction between students with and without disabilities. Efforts to free the same time period became bogged down in the same areas; there was limited free time for grade-level teachers, and the numbers and the severity of students with disabilities were disproportionate between the grade-level teachers. When the single-loop learning strategy did not produce appreciable results, the teachers used a double-loop learning process by returning the problem to core school values and beliefs.

Realizing core values helps problem-solve the situation. Double-loop learning helps the teams focus on the values that are most important to the organization and keep the decision making on a basic level. When teams are able to look at the common ground provided by core values, problem solving becomes more focused and directed than the scattered and opinionated fixes seen in single loop.

When the teachers talked about the values of the school and their personal teaching beliefs, they were able to reorganize the operations of the school in the following ways. For the next school year the classrooms that had students with specific disabilities were grouped close to each other and near the sites where the few "pull-out sessions" occurred. Teachers designated fifteen minutes every week, to start, to meet with the special education resource teacher and the classroom teachers with students with disabilities assigned to their classroom. Eventually the grade-level teachers who did not have students with disabilities helped cover the other classrooms to give teachers with students with disabilities increased time for planning.

Without going back to core values and beliefs in an honest and sincere manner this problem would probably not be resolved.

THE TRANSFORMATIONAL LEADER

The transformation leader is the leader who is initiating and directing the activities of the learning organization. The transformational leader sees a future based upon the change unit growing and developing to improve quality and effectiveness. This leader can be anyone in the change unit, or anywhere in an organizational system who wants and believes that staying put is demise and change is a necessary ingredient to success.

The transformational leader recognizes the potential all members in the organization have to contribute to the change and operations of the organization. This leader has a firm understanding of change processes, its benefits, and the concerns held by employees about change. The leader values each employee and more so appreciates the ideas, experience, and thoughts of each member and sees the relationship between the attributes of each stakeholder to the successful implementation of a learning organization.

Leading the implementation of a learning organization is really a full-time job, but it is intertwined with other duties of the leader. The transformation leader is not necessarily the school principal or the district administrator, or the president of the school board; the transformational leader can be anyone in the organization who has a future-driven quality focus.

Granted, the learning organization process seems to progress in a more organized and productive manner if the transformational leader is one with some authority and responsibility for the operation of the change unit; but not always. It has been seen in business when a transformational leader arises from the rank and file.

Leadership is not a job title, and it is not to be confused with management. Leadership is an attribute found in some people that transcends the common attitude of "just do your job." So while anyone can be a transformational leader, it does take the right person to be one. Leadership is a trait or an attribute. Leadership can also be learned, practiced, and molded to fit specific and individual organizational needs.

Transformational leadership can be found at all levels of a local education agency and on IEP teams. Leaders emerge from need, through opportunities, or by knowledge. When transformational leadership begins to emerge from a position not at the top of the organizational chart, this aspiring leader must be prepared to engage top management and major stakeholders in the transformational process to create a learning organization.

There are no rules for this engagement but one—that is persistence. The ability of the rising leader to sell, demonstrate, and rationalize its benefits will need to be done, respecting the authority and the position of top school administration and immediately including school administrators in the process.

References

Ansoff, H. I. (1987). *Corporate strategy.* New York: Penguin Publishing.

Argyris, C. (1994). *On organizational learning.* Cambridge, MA: Blackwell.

Argyris, C. and Schön, D. A. (1974). *Theory in practice: Increasing professional effectiveness.* San Francisco: Jossey-Bass.

Argyris, C. and Schön, D. A. (1996). *Organizational learning II: Theory, method, and practice.* New York: Addison-Wesley.

Armenakis, A. A., Harris, S. G. and Mossholder, K. W. (2000). Creating readiness for organizational change. In W. L. French, C. H. Bell & R. A. Zawachi (Eds.), *Organizational development and transformation: Managing effective change* (pp. 237–340). New York: Irwin McGraw-Hill.

Bennis, W. and Biedermann, P. W. (1997). *Organizing genius: The secrets of creating and leading collaboration.* Cambridge, MA: Perseus Books.

Burns, J. M. (1978). *Leadership.* New York: Harper & Row.

Ciulla, J. B. (1998). *Ethics: The heart of leadership.* Westport, CT: Quorum Books.

Dunn, M. A. (2006). *Social skills in our schools.* Shawnee Mission, KS: Autism Asperger Publishing Co.

Dunn-Buron, K. (2003). *The incredible 5-point scale.* Shawnee Mission, KS: Autism Asperger Publishing Co.

Erwin, E. J. and Soodak, L. C. (1995). I never knew I could stand up to the system: Families' perspectives on pursuing inclusive education. *Journal of the Association for Persons with Severe Handicaps*, 20, 136–146.

Fish, W. D. (2008). The IEP meeting: Perceptions of parents of students who receive special education services. *Preventing School Failure*, 53 (1), 8–15.

French, W. L. and Bell, C. H. Jr. (Eds.). (1999). *Organization development: Behavioral science interventions for organizational improvement.* Upper Saddle River, NJ: Prentice-Hall.

Garvin, D. A. (1993). Building a learning organization. In W. L. French, C. H. Bell, Jr. & R. A. Zawacki (Eds.). *Organization development and transformation: Managing effective change* (pp. 281–94). New York: Irwin McGraw-Hill.

Greenleaf, R. K. (1977). *Servant leadership: A journey into the nature of legitimate power and greatness*. New York: Paulist.

Lentz, K. W. (2004). *Hopes and dreams: An IEP guide for parents of children with autism spectrum disorders*. Shawnee Mission, KS: Autism Asperger Publishing Co.

Lewin, K. (1958). Group decisions and social change. In E. E. Maccoby, T.M. Newcomb & E. L. Hartley (Eds.). *Readings in social psychology*. Oxford, UK: Henry Holt.

McGill, M. E. and Slocum, J. W. Jr. (1994). *The smarter organization: How to build a business that learns and adapts to marketplace needs*. New York: John Wiley.

Pruitt, D., Wandry, D., & Hollums, D. (1988). Listen to us! Parents speak out about their interactions with special educators. *Preventing School Failure*, 42, 161–166.

Rost, J. C. (1991). *Leadership for the 21st century*. Westport, CT: Praeger.

Schein, E. H. (1996). Culture: The missing concept in organizational studies. *Administrative Science Quarterly*, 41, 229–40.

Schein, E. H. (2010). *Organizational culture and leadership*, 4th edition. Hoboken, NJ: John Wiley and Sons.

Senge, P. M. (1990). *The fifth discipline: The art and practice of the learning organization*. New York: Currency Doubleday.

Sergiovanni, T. J. (1992). *Moral leadership*. San Francisco: Jossey-Bass.

Sheppard, B. and Brown, J. (2000). So you think team leadership is easy? Training and implementation concerns. *NASSP Bulletin*, 84, 21–83.

Spears, L. C. (Ed.) (1998). *The power of servant leadership*. San Francisco: Berret-Koehler Publishers.

Index

About the Author

With forty years' experience working with students and adults having autism; behavioral/emotional disorders; learning disabilities; and speech, hearing, and visual limitations, **Kirby Lentz** has led thousands of IEP teams to meet meaningful student outcomes. He has served as CEO for a specialized school, was a member and past president of a local school board, worked on a variety of local and state committees and task forces, and is a parent of a child with exceptional needs. Dr. Lentz is an adjunct instructor at Viterbo University

He received his doctorate in educational leadership, with an emphasis on organizational development and effectiveness, from Saint Mary's University in Minneapolis. He is the author of *Hopes and Dreams: A Guide for Parents Having Children with ASD.*

Born and raised in the Philadelphia area, Lentz and his wife, BJ, reside in Wisconsin. They have three adult children and four outstanding grandchildren (who doesn't at our age?). Visit on the web at www.lentzsolutions.com or check in on the Lentz Blog at http://lentzsolutions.wordpress.com.

CPSIA information can be obtained at www.ICGtesting.com
Printed in the USA
BVOW041705090512

289748BV00004BA/2/P